ACTION LEARNING
Images and Pathways

The Professional Practices in Adult Education and Lifelong Learning Series explores issues and concerns of practitioners who work in the broad range of settings in adult and continuing education and lifelong learning.

The books provide information and strategies on how to make practice more effective for professionals and those they serve. They are written from a practical viewpoint and provide a forum for instructors, administrators, policy makers, counselors, trainers, instructional designers, and other related professionals. The series contains single author or coauthored books only and does not include edited volumes.

Sharan B. Merriam
Ronald M. Cervero
Series Editors

ACTION LEARNING
Images and Pathways

Robert L. Dilworth
Verna J. Willis

With foreword by
Reginald W. Revans

KRIEGER PUBLISHING COMPANY
Malabar, Florida
2003

Original Edition 2003

Printed and Published by
**KRIEGER PUBLISHING COMPANY
KRIEGER DRIVE
MALABAR, FLORIDA 32950**

Copyright © 2003 by Robert L. Dilworth and Verna J. Willis

All rights reserved. No part of this book may be reproduced in any form or by any means, electronic or mechanical, including information storage and retrieval systems without permission in writing from the publisher.
No liability is assumed with respect to the use of the information contained herein.
Printed in the United States of America.

FROM A DECLARATION OF PRINCIPLES JOINTLY ADOPTED BY A COMMITTEE OF THE AMERICAN BAR ASSOCIATION AND A COMMITTEE OF PUBLISHERS:

This publication is designed to provide accurate and authoritative information in regard to the subject matter covered. It is sold with the understanding that the publisher is not engaged in rendering legal, accounting, or other professional service. If legal advice or other expert assistance is required, the services of a competent professional person should be sought.

Library of Congress Cataloging-in-Publication Data

Dilworth, Robert L. (Robert Lex), 1936–
    Action learning : images and pathways / Robert L. Dilworth, Verna J. Willis ; with foreword by Reginald W. Revans. — Original ed.
      p. cm. — (The professional practices in adult education and lifelong learning series)
    Includes bibliographical references and index.
    ISBN 1-57524-203-6 (hard : alk. paper)
    1. Active learning. 2. Adult education. 3. Continuing education.
I. Willis, Verna J., 1926– II. Title. III. Series.
LB1027.23 .D57 2003
374—dc21   2002027582

10   9   8   7   6   5   4   3   2

CONTENTS

Foreword by Reginald W. Revans	vii
Preface	xi
Acknowledgments	xvii
The Authors	xxi
1. The Nature of Action Learning	1
2. Action Learning in Various Contexts	33
3. Contextual Implications of Action Learning: Lessons Learned	56
4. The Action Learning Plan	78
5. Phases of the Action Learning Cycle	102
6. Action Learning in Various Domains, Contexts, and Cultures	126
7. The Transformative Potential of Action Learning	152
8. Reflections on How To Bring It All Together	172
Glossary	187
References	193
Index	197

FOREWORD

When Professors Lex Dilworth and Verna Willis were asked to write this book, they built upon existing years of mutual collaboration—and in undertaking this joint task they continued to learn with and from each other. They drew upon their practical experience—where again they had "learnt with and from" others—from doing the thing rather than just writing about it. Most books are written to gratify some need of the author, who then works hard to contrive publication. Some books are written to explore an idea, and publication is of little subsequent interest. And a few works are written at the behest of third parties, who wanted to see placed on record and disseminated the understanding, or questioning insight, which they perceived would be of benefit to others. This book lies firmly and refreshingly in the latter category. It is neither an exercise in self-gratification, self-promotion, nor commercial gain. It is instead the work of people who were asked to share with others their insight into certain aspects of Action Learning so that we may all learn together with and from each other. If all books were written and published in this spirit we might all be saved a lot of confusion and irrelevance.

What is also notable is the differing backgrounds of my two friends—and that despite or because of this they have been able to collaborate and learn even the more from each other. Doubtless they will explain herein how this simply represents an increased breadth of "Q" as well as "P."

Action Learning is now pursued in many countries around the world—from America to Australia, from Sweden to South Africa, from Romania to Uganda, and most places in between. I have visited the majority of the countries myself these last seven decades—though at 94 years of age I recognize that my globe-trotting days are now over. But when speaking about Action Learning I have always insisted that people can only learn of Action Learning by practicing Action Learning. And that the students or "fellows" of Action Learning must engage with the real "here and now" of reality. This is what happened in the late 1960s in what has become known as the "Belgian Project." It is encouraging that our authors follow that example so closely—indeed perhaps closer than any others—by insisting that their own Action Learners go into the real world and tackle real problems in real organizations, with real consequences. None of Dr. Dilworth's nor Dr. Willis's sets are allowed to become dependent on the tuition of others. Mentorship is always at hand, but is forthcoming only when truly justified. It is not an "easy option." The sets are not allowed to become reliant upon facilitators nor advisors, either. For the focus is not about teaching—it is about *learning*—together!

This learning process is also critically about the Self. Unless this aspect of change has also been addressed, then there can have been little truly worthwhile learning at all. It was Gaston Deurinck who noted the question to which all the participants of the Belgian Project later subscribed as being the most important question they had learnt to ask themselves: "What is an honest man, and what need I do to become one?" So apart from reversing the downward spiral of the Belgian economy at that time, the participants each addressed the problems of their own value systems. The learning was critically within themselves as well as without—and they could not achieve the latter change without addressing the former.

The fundamental difference in perspective—which we must emphasize most strongly—is also the hallmark of the difference between "cleverness" and "wisdom." It also parallels the difference between knowledge and understanding where the knowledge can originate from reading, studying, hypothesizing, and writing—whilst understanding demands activity, test, experiment, the doing of practical deeds, and engagement with reality.

We noted years ago that " . . . to understand an idea one must be able to apply it in practice, and to understand a situation, one must be able to change it." Verbal description is not comment enough. It is from consistently replicated and successful practice that is distilled and concentrated the knowledge we describe as successful theory. The process by which one is transformed into the other is the scientific method, and the essence of the scientific method is the experimental test: Are the results using the theory in practice substantially the results we predicted? . . . The essence of the experimental test is to compare achievement with anticipation; it is the feedback on which the science of cybernetics is built. Thus, the theory of practice is the ring on which all the keys of the human intelligence are assembled. So practice is the essential ingredient to learning about Action Learning—and our authors have eschewed any approach which chains the process to the classroom or lecture hall.

I have known Lex Dilworth and Verna Willis for many years and have enjoyed constant communication—and visits from them whenever possible. They are true collaborators. The questions which they pose and the scenarios which provide the background to their observations are essentially the same as those which can also be traced in the pages of Genesis. Even then our human frailty was such that arrogance claimed that the route to heaven could be reached by a large tower, bypassing integrity of personal effort by reliance upon technique alone. When in those days the consequence of fantasy was babble and confusion—do we even today find similar consequences when we ignore human qualities in favour of "techniques" born in ivory towers and sterile studies isolated from the realities of the practicing world? Our authors do not live in such a remote world of fantasy—they are firmly in touch with reality, and this distinguishes them from most other contributors.

In my study in Tilstock I have recently added upwards of one thousand books. One thing strikes me as readily apparent: that most authors display their knowledge by writing—but that writing doesn't offer any real understanding unless it is fortified by practical experience. You can write a book about riding a bicycle without being able to ride a bicycle. You can explain balance, vector control, energy usage, speed effect, friction drag, air resistance, and other scientific aspects. But writing about riding a bicycle or reading about riding a bicycle is not sufficient—for whilst this supplies knowledge, it does not provide understanding. Only by actually riding a bicycle will one *understand* how it is done. Now as far as Action Learning is concerned, Professors Dilworth and Willis understand well—because, unlike many other authors, they have actually done it, and not just written and talked about it.

Professor Reg Revans
Tilstock—May 2001

PREFACE

This book represents the continuation of a quest, one centered on bringing to the human experience the opportunity for people to learn with and from each other. As the adult educator and philosopher Eduard Lindeman once said, "Learning is coterminus with life." However, all too often the learning experiences offered by our school systems and universities center on formal learning, where one-way lecturing is the delivery means of choice. This didactic approach reinforces the dependency of learners, rather than encouraging them to think and problem solve independently, the very skills that they will ultimately require to be successful in life.

Alternatively, action learning strikes us as a sleeping giant in the catalogue of individual and organizational change strategies. It has been around and talked about for over half a century, yet many have not heard of it, or if they have, have viewed it as just another variant of "learning by doing." It is distinctly more than that. It has the potential for putting control of lifelong learning directly in the hands of learners in ways that alter their perceptions, amplify self-efficacy, and reconnect these individuals to spontaneous curiosity and confidence in the exercise of their own good judgment. Using action learning in education, in business, and in other social institutions is like turning on think tanks everywhere without losing either the concern for others or the action focus that gets things done.

Learners need ownership in the learning agenda, especially when they become adults. The answer is to balance the formal learning experience with informal learning, where the learners not only interact with the instructor, but with each other. To the extent the interaction is focused on something that is relevant and engages with the real world, the learning experience is enhanced. This is the niche that action learning fills so well.

To unleash ethical individual growth and development without sacrificing the strengths of community seems more urgent than ever in this millennium. There are multiple forces that seem aligned against this proposition. Not only do we still have the legacy of teacher-directed learning and facilitator-controlled group processes, we also have the new challenges of making solo-operated technology community-friendly in a global society so close to us that we often cannot see the forest for the trees.

In every institution there are pressures to do more with less, to come up with metrics that prove we are faster, smarter, more culturally sensitive, and more valuable as human "producers" than ever before. We have become obsessed with just-in-time everything—the epitome of efficiency that even dictates how our minds will work.

Our experience with action learning has convinced us that it is a modality well suited to the times. Engagement with real problems, as opposed to prefabricated ones, becomes the engine that induces deep learning. It is a case of balancing action with inquiry and reflection. In this regard, action learning shares common roots with action research. It is also a case of acting, after adequate diagnosis, and then reflecting on what occurred before correcting the form of action and trying again. Marvin Weisbord, in writing about action research and the contribution made by Kurt Lewin, states that:

> Lewin intended his enhanced problem-solving model to preserve democratic values, build commitment to act, and motivate learning—all at once. Indeed some people have renamed the process "action learning" to more accurately indicate its nature. (1987, p. 187)

While action learning shares important roots with action research, it also has sprung from the way scientists behave as they work purposefully in their laboratories, confronting the unknown day after day. We will point out some of the very important ways in which action learning differs from action research. One difference is the degree of emphasis on the learning component and the importance of critical reflection to the process. The outcomes that result often relate to personal growth and a greatly enhanced ability to deal with complicated problems.

In the course of our work with action learning we have heard over and over, in the learners' own words, that for the first time in their lives they have felt "free to learn." Since we have both done a lot of teaching, formal and informal, to hear this is something of a shock, and yet it underscores the catalytic value of action learning. What is it about learning done previously that has made them feel so un-free? And what is it about action learning that breeds thoughtful but almost immediate action to change some problem situation that seemed insurmountable? Why is it that action learners begin very quickly to act out the proposition that they can change the course of their lives, their organizations, their communities, and their world?

This book aims to supply some of the answers to these questions, but above all, it seeks to enable those who are interested to try action learning for themselves. Difficult to define, experienced very personally, action learning does not become transparent overnight. A great deal depends on context, so that we cannot prescribe a single right way to proceed with the action learning process. Nevertheless, there are guidelines that experience and conversations with our colleagues tell us will be helpful for new start-ups, and there are pitfalls we can tell you about that can be avoided. We gladly share what we know and what we still have questions about. We make no claims to perfect wisdom. Our students keep telling us that, as fascinated as they are by the learning yield and the way it happens, they, too, have trouble getting their arms around this thing called action learning.

Action learning is increasingly being used as a learning strategy of choice in our largest corporations in the United States and around the world. Marquardt suggests that action learning simultaneously meets the five most important needs facing organizations today: problem solving, organizational learning, leadership development, professional growth, and career development (1999, p. 5). It appeals to corporations and other institutions precisely because it can unearth clues to some of the organization's most pressing problems. There can be a significant payback tactically as soon as a present-day issue is resolved anywhere in the organization. Strategically, action learning positions the organization for future challenges by building the capacities and competencies of those in the workforce.

With all the perceived benefits of action learning, one might believe that it would spread like wildfire. While it is making greater inroads all the time, there are often barriers to implementation. Some are linked to the way power is distributed in the organization. Action learning can be perceived as a threat to the power base because of its emphasis on enabling and empowering workers. Middle managers can see their authoritative leverage reduced, as employees deal more directly with problems and decide for themselves how to resolve them. There is a case of a major corporation that pursued action learning full bore and told the workforce that they would find themselves empowered to take action. The employees believed this executive announcement and proceeded to fully live up to the process that had been put in place. The top leadership became concerned when employees acted on the opportunity and began to challenge established practices. The program was quickly quashed. Those who work in other settings will jump in immediately to say that corporations are not the only places where such quashing goes on.

Action learning turns out to be an approach to both learning and management of people that is in tune with the times. The diffusion of organizational power (moving from hierarchical to heterarchical) and emphasis on solutions engineered by those closest to the problem mesh comfortably with action learning. There is a dawning recognition that "expert" solutions don't necessarily work in a time of rapid change, where solutions to today's problems may well fall outside the solution sets that were in vogue yesterday. But that does not make introduction of action learning easy. It breaks with the more traditional ways of managing organizations and leading people. It can also be viewed by those in the human resource development (HRD) profession, including professional trainers, as an approach that can put them out of business. Fears among human resource developers are reinforced by the number of training departments being closed down in favor of e-learning delivery methods and adoption of experiential approaches to learning. The rapid growth of corporate universities is another challenge, especially since action learning is one means such universities are turning to for management development.

Earlier books on action learning have for the most part devoted almost exclusive attention to the business sector. This book corrects for the neglect of literature on action learning in other settings. Because the corporation has been the focus, little attention has been given to the shaping of action learning in very different organizational cultures or to the biases that discipline specific and professional education have unwittingly introduced in different contexts. Consequently, we have several additional audiences in mind for this book.

Adult education and HRD professors often ask how to go about incorporating action learning in the academic setting. We offer action learning through capstone courses that take our students outside the university and thrust them into the heart of organizational crises. We will say much more about this later.

We have initiated action learning in major corporations, small businesses, a Romanian hospital, an African college of technology, a church, government agencies, and a school district, to name a few of the constituent groups where we have found interest, commitment, and a readership for any materials we can provide them. Further, we are aware of action learning applications in e-business, social work, communities and community colleges, and nongovernment agencies (NGOs). We believe that wherever adult education is undertaken, action learning can help to establish a profoundly effective "learning habit" that can be sustained throughout life. It has also been used in high schools, so we cannot assume that it is solely an adult education prerogative.

In Chapter 1, "The Nature of Action Learning," we introduce its origins, the governing philosophy, and the basic principles and requirements. Links among action learning, adult education, and learning at the rate of change are clarified.

Chapter 2, "Action Learning in Various Contexts," suggests 5 domains of practice and 16 contexts. Dominant assumptions and mindsets that influence acceptance and applications of action learning in different venues are considered. In Chapter 3, "Contextual Implications of Action Learning: Lessons Learned," we take a closer look at ways to gain commitment to the action learning process and ensure its success.

Chapter 4, "The Action Learning Plan," gets specific about selecting models, optimizing diversity, establishing time frames, identifying the problem, and specifying the terms of client participation. Chapter 5, "Phases of the Action Learning Cycle," explores the iterative nature of action learning and the issues of implementation encountered.

Chapter 6, "Action Learning in Various Domains, Contexts, and Cultures," summarizes and comments upon the driving forces and restraining forces that may either assist or hinder the application of action learning in specific contexts. In Chapter 7, "The Transformative Potential of Action Learning," outcomes that go far beyond cognitive knowledge gains are claimed. This chapter is essentially derived from the ongoing research studies of the authors.

Chapter 8, "Reflections on How to Bring It All Together," is intended to be a quick, convenient debriefing, with checklists and reminders, tips on customization of programs, and specific pointers for dealing with diverse set compositions and diverse settings. We hope this will turn the tide and strengthen your resolve to venture into at least the wading pool end of action learning.

A glossary of the most significant action learning terms is included.

ACKNOWLEDGMENTS

This book has been developed out of the knowledge gained from many people, including associates in action learning over the years from Great Britain, South Africa, Sweden, Romania, China, India, Zambia, Australia, and the Côte d' Ivoire. Towering over all the others is Reginald W. Revans of England, action learning's lodestar for over 50 years. His involvement with action learning in over 60 countries and his extensive research and writings on the subject have earned him the title of "Father of Action Learning." His work was our constant reference point throughout the book development.

Lex met Reg in 1991 through Victoria Marsick of Columbia University. He ended up gaining a dear friend, frequent colleague, and mentor. Along the way, Verna came to know Reg and became a trusted and close colleague as well.

In 1995 the first Action Learning and Mutual Collaboration Congress was held at Heathrow, England. Twenty nations were represented. Some already close associations were strengthened as a result of the Congress, and new associations forged. We think of the late Lord John Butterfield, who through his personal support made the Congress possible. Reg Revans personally subsidized the travel of a number of representatives from developing countries that otherwise would not have been able to participate. In this Congress, other major contributors to knowledge of the nature of action learning were Albert Barker of England, Neil McAdam of Australia, and David Botham, who currently serves as Director of the Revans Institute for Action Learning and Research at the University of Salford in England.

Among others with whom we have also had important dialogue about action learning are Alan Mumford, Krystyna Weinstein, Janet Craig, John Morris, and Mike Pedler of the

United Kingdom, Michael Marquardt of George Washington University, Annie Brooks of the University of Texas, and Victoria Marsick of Columbia University. We value their insights.

Understanding that systems thinking and action learning are natural partners has grown from old and new associations with general system theorists, human relations training pioneers, and management scholars whose names would be easily recognized by most of our readers. These influential thinkers, many of whom we have personally known, constitute such a long list that we would err grossly on the side of omission to name even a few of them. But we cannot let their contributions go completely unnoted.

Beyond Reg Revans, two scholars need to be singled out for special mention. The first is Albert Barker, already mentioned. He encouraged this book, recognizing that it represented an opportunity to outline the characteristics of action learning in a way that traveled back to the very roots of action learning as developed by Revans. The second person has for the most part had little direct involvement with action learning. However, he has influenced this book in important ways. We want to recognize Jack Mezirow, Professor Emeritus at Teachers College, Columbia University. We have repeatedly encountered transformative learning as an outcome of action learning. Jack's work as one of the stellar adult educators in the world and perhaps the foremost voice on transformative learning, has had significant impact on this book.

There have been legions of graduate students over the years who have come to recognize the value of action learning, and even found their lives transformed by it. Both of us have learned a great deal through the experiences these men and women have shared with us. To all the others we have encountered who have advanced our knowledge of action learning, we also say heartfelt thanks. We know through them that action learning is a matter of great interest to a great many people.

Our appreciation goes to Sharan Merriam and Ron Cervero for their generous and incisive editorial guidance. Mary Roberts of Krieger Publishing Company was a pleasure to deal with as

Acknowledgments xix

we launched the book and then worked it through its final editorial stages.

Finally we want to acknowledge each other. Without the stimulus of earnest dialogue throughout the writing process (marked by questioning inquiry, the Q so valued by Reg Revans), the book would not have been completed. Our families, too, have been more patient and helpful than outsiders could ever imagine; children have thoughtfully relinquished claims on our time. Doris Dilworth is especially appreciated as key supporter and helpmate for Lex in fulfilling responsibilities to the book.

This is a book about capitalizing on synergy, and it has taken all of us to get this book to you. We hope everyone will be the richer for it.

THE AUTHORS

Robert L. (Lex) Dilworth is Associate Professor of Adult Education and Human Resource Development in the graduate program of the School of Education at Virginia Commonwealth University. He received his doctorate in adult and continuing education from Columbia University in 1993. He earned a master's degree in military art and science from the U.S. Army's Command and General Staff College in 1972, a master's degree in public administration from the University of Oklahoma in 1995, and an MA in education from Columbia University in 1992. When he graduated from the University of Florida in 1959 with a BS in advertising, he concurrently became an officer in the U.S. Army. He has also completed advanced management programs at Harvard University, Northwestern University, the University of Michigan, and the Industrial College of the Armed Forces.

He retired from the U.S. Army in 1991 as a brigadier general, having served as the 54th The Adjutant General of the U.S. Army, a position that gave him responsibility for overseeing Army personnel systems worldwide. He was able to spend considerable time experimenting with organizations, including major involvement with organization development (OD). Before his first formal introduction to action learning in 1990, he was in effect practicing this modality.

From 1991 to 1993, he headed the Bureau of Human Resource Management and Development for Florida's Department of Labor and Employment Security.

Dilworth has a special interest in the global arena and cross-cultural awareness and sensitivity. He has also done extensive research in the area of adult literacy and basic skills. His experience includes consulting with companies in a variety of areas, including action learning, through his consulting firm, Strategic Learning Scenarios.

Verna J. Willis is Associate Professor of Human Resource Development (HRD) in the Andrew Young School of Policy Studies at Georgia State University in Atlanta, Georgia, where in 1989 she established award-winning HRD degree programs. The BS, MS and PhD programs are located in the Department of Public Administration and Urban Studies.

Willis teaches that the multidisciplinary field of HRD is best represented as a dynamic, evolutionary system of thought and practice. She originated the Chief Learning Officer concept, making a business case for placing learning leadership in organizations at executive team level.

Willis received a PhD in education at the State University of New York at Buffalo in 1977. Her BA (1964) and MA (1967) degrees in English literature and education were earned at Alfred University, Alfred, New York. From 1972 to 1976 she was training director for the New York State and Erie County Center for Human Services Training, funded to prepare career ladder paraprofessionals for work in 60 community mental health agencies. Willis supported doctoral studies by teaching in a variety of school settings in the Buffalo area, including middle and secondary schools, community and four-year colleges, and SUNYAB.

Willis was employed by the Ministry of Education in Doha, Qatar, to assist with implementing and evaluating a new ESL curriculum (1978–1980) and spent 1987–88 as a World Bank consultant to higher education institutions in Indonesia. She managed corporate training and development at M & T Bank in Buffalo between these overseas postings.

To understand and lead organizational change, she has worked with the National Training Laboratories organization development network and many management consulting firms. Willis consults with private, nonprofit, and public organizations, to encourage systems thinking and action learning initiatives.

CHAPTER 1

The Nature of Action Learning

In any epoch of rapid change those organizations unable to adapt are soon in trouble, and adaptation is only achieved by learning, namely by being able to do tomorrow that which might have been unnecessary today, or be able to do today what was unnecessary last week . . . Action learning takes up from the start the need to help managers—and all others who engage in it—acquire this insight into the posing of questions by the simple device of setting them to tackle real problems that have so far defied solution.
—Reginald W. Revans (1983, p. 11)

    Action learning is full of surprises. Far from being a process where prespecified outcomes lead to predictable thoughts and behaviors, it is often in the reversal of expectations that its real strength lies. Rather than begin by explaining action learning in terms of principles, rules, and frameworks, as so often occurs in defining an approach, technique or concept, we choose to reverse that order and begin with three examples of tackling real problems, working forward from there. Each example tells a story that offers a glimpse into the "uncertainty logic" of action learning.
    Reg Revans, deservedly called the "Father of Action Learning," speaks of the essence of action learning as being quite simple, yet all too often it gets clouded over with attempts to explain it in traditional ways. It is as if any concept that is seen as possessing powerful properties from the standpoint of management of organizations must have a complex analytical construct

associated with it to underwrite its validity. Action learning, in the end, is as natural as living life itself, and the power of action learning is in understanding some of the basics that bring it about. It also has demonstrable links to adult learning theory.

FINDING OUR WAY THROUGH EXAMPLES

Example 1. The Computer Response Problem

In 1991, Dilworth headed a large organization with nationwide responsibilities. Much of the work of the organization involved the use of computer networks. One day he noticed that his own computer hesitated for a moment or two in moving between screen images. This was not a new phenomenon, but at that particular moment Dilworth recognized that if this were true across his organization, given the tens of thousands of computer-related transactions dealt with daily, that it represented a major drag weight on productivity. When he inspected other computer-equipment in the organization, he found the same systemic shortfall.

At that point he called in his information technology specialists and brought the problem to their attention. They said it was fixable, even a "piece of cake." They committed to work on it. Three weeks later, the in-house experts confessed that they were stumped. Representatives from the major computer firm (a Fortune 500 company) servicing the equipment were called in. After an hour of problem diagnosis, they reported that it was a fixable problem but would require a $6 million upgrade. There was an arrogance, a "take it or leave it" attitude on the part of these computer experts. Dilworth drafted a letter to the chief executive officer (CEO) of the computer company outlining his high level of dissatisfaction with the service being provided and an expression of intent to shift the business to a competitor if that was the best they could do.

The following Monday when Dilworth arrived at work,

The Nature of Action Learning

three company experts were waiting to see him. They had been flown in at the direction of their CEO. After a half-day of investigating the problem, they reported that the earlier diagnosis had been correct. It would cost $6 million to correct the problem. That left a couple of obvious options. One option was to simply accept the computer system's inefficiency; the other option was to accept the diagnosis of the experts and seek $6 million to do the system upgrade.

In the end, a very different option was selected. There were 22 management interns (trainees) in the organization, scattered throughout 14 different suborganizations. Most of the individuals had never worked together before and only two were being developed to be computer experts. None of them had ever done any major computer troubleshooting. Beyond the two interns who were in the process of developing very strong computer skills, the rest were undergoing various stages of basic computer literacy training. What they did have going for them was high intelligence. Interns had been selected for the management internship based on their high potential.

Dilworth assembled the interns and explained the situation to them, including the fact that the experts had dismissed the problem as unsolvable without a major expenditure of funds. Would they be willing to take a look at the problem, and then try to solve it as a learning experience? After a brief caucus, they said, "Yes." One intern commented, "It cannot get any worse than it is." The group was assured that they would receive top management backing and should feel fully empowered. The interns had an organizational meeting a few days later. The in-house computer experts showed up unexpectedly and offered their assistance. One intern said, "Did you solve the problem?" The answer was "no." The computer experts were then invited to leave, with a request that they remain on call should the interns need them. Some in the organization commented about the unfairness of giving a group of management trainees such a daunting task. To them it seemed unfair and illogical.

A month later, the computer problem had been fixed at no cost beyond the time the interns had spent troubleshooting the problem. The interns, truly "nonexperts," then presented their findings to a conference room packed with people, including the computer experts from the major computer company. What the interns outlined can be summed up as follows:

1. The experts were looking in the wrong places for a solution. The problem was not caused by a single major driver, but rather by a wide array of factors. When each of these variations was brought under control, they collectively led to a major system turnaround.
2. The interns found sister organizations to have the same problem. While they were about it, they fixed those problems as well. They had recognized that if systems external to their own organization were inefficient they impacted the responsiveness of the entire network.
3. The time expenditure to work on the problem was expected to be paid back within six months in terms of greater computer system efficiency and productivity (Dilworth, 1998, pp. 31–32).

Example 2. The Power Generation Problem

Florida Power & Light found itself with a problem of roughly 10 years standing in the late 1980s. They were experiencing a significant loss in terms of electricity being generated in relation to what ended up with the consumer. Various experts and task forces within the company had been charged with solving the problem, but they had been unsuccessful. They then brought together a hybrid team of individuals from across the company, a group that had not been involved with this particular type of problem before. In a matter of months, they had solved the problem. As was true with the earlier computer example, the team found a variety of causal factors. When a variety of fixes were aggregated, it led to a major systems improvement. One of the contributing factors they found was birds on power lines. The bird droppings could short out lines. Like the computer team in the first example, the power generation team (they came to call themselves "The Drips" and wore tee shirts so inscribed) were very proud of their accomplishment and professed to having learned a great deal (Dilworth, 1998, p. 33).

Example 3. The Truck Problem

A five-ton military truck broke down on a remote road in South Korea. A fuel line had broken. The three low-ranking U.S. Army soldiers with the truck did not have a tool set that allowed them to readily deal with such repairs. It was something you dealt with in a fully equipped automotive maintenance facility. They would obviously have to live by their wits if they were to get the vehicle back on the road. They had an intense discussion. They had to get the truck back to their camp by sundown. After inventorying what they had available to make repairs (much as Robinson Crusoe must have done), they settled on a course of action.

The soldiers had a large can of vegetables. They cut out both ends with a can opener and emptied out the contents. They created a makeshift sleeve over the break in the fuel line using the can. They crimped it as tightly as they could by hand and using a set of pliers. They then wrapped duct tape and baling wire around it to more fully secure the tin patch on the line. It worked. The truck started up and they roared off.

ORIGINS AND GOVERNING PHILOSOPHY OF ACTION LEARNING

What these three examples have in common is related directly to the nature of action learning. None of the examples described was labeled at the time as being action learning related, but each, in its own way, brings to life the uncertain conditions that prompt action learning and express what action learning is really about. Several action learning specific lessons can be drawn from the three examples:

1. People learn best from and with each other.
2. The learner has the central role in setting the specific agenda for action learning.
3. Action learning occurs best in an atmosphere of trust and mutual support.
4. Real problems are the greatest impetus for learning and the more daunting they are, the greater the impetus can be.
5. Fresh questions are induced most readily when the problem being dealt with is unfamiliar and there are many uncertainties.
6. Action learners need to start with the problem at hand and what is happening, not with formulas for problem scoping developed for yesterday's problems

The origins of action learning, in Revans's view, go back thousands of years. Certainly there are many historical events and happenings that tend to approximate the examples already provided. Revans identifies his own involvement with the rigor and knowledge seeking of scientific discovery as a major influence on his conception and practice of action learning. Revans names three systems—Alpha, Beta, and Gamma—which are interwoven and collectively form the core of the action learning process (Revans, 1971, pp. 33-67; 1970, pp. 141-161; 1982, pp. 330-347). The "habit of science" and the associated "habit of systems thinking" contribute to the governing philosophy of action learning.

For Revans, any scientist with integrity will first of all choose to work on a problem that has a significant, real impact on people (System Alpha). That problem will yield to understanding only if thoroughly investigated in all of its ramifications, through many tests and experiments that are then subject to review and revision (System Beta). The scientist is honor-bound throughout the entire breadth and depth of the inquiry to assess and reassess what is being learned and what the consequences of that learning are for self and others (System Gamma). For

Revans, critical self-reflection is simply part and parcel of being a conscientious scientist.

In the 1940s, Revans in the United Kingdom and Lewin in the United States were concerned with many of the same kinds of social issues, and were both looking for new, effective ways to address them. Lewin was himself a trained scientist whose field theory of personality is (like Revans's theory of action learning) based on dynamics occurring within systems (Hall & Lindzey, 1970, pp. 209–257). He undertook with others to alleviate human problems through understanding of group behavior, and as a further evolution, through an inquiry process akin to action research. Lewin had much to do with the genesis of a group process used now for harnessing the power of action learning. Action research and action learning share some things in common. Both focus on action, and then reflection on action, before taking further action. However, as will be shown, action learning has other qualities that distinguish it from action research.

The reflective component can be seen in action science, where what has occurred is subject to careful review and reflection. The U.S. Army, and other organizations, are finding that an "after action review process," grounded in deep introspection, can lead to important revelations. The famous World War II German general, Erwin Rommel, understood the power of reflection. When he was a lieutenant in World War I, he would sit down on a tree stump or riverbank after a battle and carefully take stock of what had occurred, and what he could learn from it (Rommel, 1979).

Revans tells stories from his own life that warn of misleading assumptions that later prove faulty, and that emphasize the learning to be gained from reflecting on one's own experiences. He recalls the *Titanic* disaster. He was only a small child but impressions were indelible. Revans's father was His Majesty's Principal Surveyor of Shipping and had been involved in the inquiry related to the disaster. In later years, he told Reg that he had learned one powerful lesson from that inquiry, and it was that "There is a big difference between cleverness and wisdom." Had there been more wisdom on the bridge the night the ship sank, the ship might have been saved. The evasive maneuvers taken to avoid the iceberg, in effect, worked against the design features of the ship that had been engineered to protect it in case of a head-on collision. Because the ship was placed at an angle to the iceberg, the side was exposed and a majority of the compartments designed to maintain the ship's integrity in a head-on collision collapsed, dooming the ship.

Revans marks his own connection with action learning as occurring when he was studying for his doctoral dissertation under J. J. Thomason, father of the electron and a Nobel prize winner. More than a dozen current or future Nobel Laureates worked in the Cavendish Laboratories where Revans did his research. Revans was struck by the dynamics of a meeting that occurred each week among these extraordinary scientists. Thomason would invite the scientists to let their guard down and openly share both progress being made and the frustrations of failure.

> That spirit was one of struggle with the unknown, the bartering of ignorance, the quest to uncover another layer of particle physics only to find themselves confronted with even greater mysteries. (Barker, 1998, p. 12)

Because physics was moving in the direction of developing weapons of mass destruction, Revans turned his attention to other pursuits, becoming an educator, and ending up on the management faculty at the University of Manchester in England. Beginning in the mid-1940s, Revans began to develop his philosophy of and theoretical premises for action learning. He spent time in the collieries, underground, with miners as they worked the coal faces. He observed that when small teams of miners were allowed to set their own priorities and agenda, their productivity far exceeded that of miners not similarly empowered.

Revans was deeply interested in the effects of working group size on employee learning and productivity. E. F. Schumacher's text, *Small Is Beautiful: A Study of Economics As If People Mattered* (1973), and his own ongoing research led him to conclude that "small is dutiful," that is, an organizational necessity (Revans, 1980, p. 103). Things can be made to happen best in small groups. Revans recommended that a staff college be created to allow dialogue around the management of mines, including the opportunity for miners to have more say in their work routines. It encountered resistance and was never brought to fruition.

Revans also became interested in the health service and hospitals. That led to a study of London's 10 largest hospitals. Problems that encouraged the need for study were high mortality rates, long hospital stays, and low staff morale. Revans designed a program allowing staff in one hospital, in small groups (later called action learning sets), to visit other hospitals to look at their operating systems. This placed the staff in a position of visiting an environment other than their own, and, in some cases, examining hospital systems remote from their own expertise. This was called the Hospital Intercommunication (HIC) Study. Implementation of the resulting recommendations led to a major drop in mortality rate in participating hospitals, shorter hospital stays, and vastly improved employee morale, reflected in a lower attrition rate.

Revans's most monumental effort involving action learning occurred in Belgium in the 1960s. Revans spent about 10 years working with a consortium of universities and industries to improve the Belgian economy. The specifics of this long-running experiment will be explained later, but, fundamentally, senior executives were sent to investigate problems at companies other than their own in areas essentially unfamiliar to them. A very large segment of the Belgian industrial base ended up participating in this effort. The results were striking. A number of persistent problems in various companies ended up being corrected.

DEFINITION AND CHARACTERISTICS

In considering the power of action learning as a concept, as allied to action research, Weisbord says:

> Few concepts have ever been so simple or so powerful. Yet the road map is not the kind you buy in Rand McNally. There are no visual keys for cities, airports, or interchanges, no measuring

scales in miles or kilometers. Indeed our perceptions of the terrain keep changing as we involve more people and learn more about each situation. (1987, p. 187)

As Revans suggests, and the practice of action learning validates, action learning is highly eclectic. In this respect it is like adult education and organization development, with which action learning shares territory. Those engaged with action learning become necessarily cross-disciplinary. There are threads of adult learning theory, management science, psychology, behavioral and laboratory science, anthropology, systems theory, and cybernetics in evidence, to name only a few.

Revans has resisted requests to define action learning, being more inclined to describe it in terms of what it is not. He does not consider the solving of puzzles, evaluation of case studies, lecture-driven classroom instruction, or simulations to be action learning. He considers them to be fabrications of reality, bound up in the past and lacking the force or relevance of present and future realities.

> ... Revans, although quite prepared to offer some comments on the necessary structure and techniques, is more concerned to avoid giving simplistic cookbook or technique illustrations. Perhaps this is why it is actually difficult to find in the writing of Revans, or indeed most other authors in this area, any agreed neat memorable definition of action learning. (Mumford, 1985, p. 1)

Perhaps as close as Revans comes to defining action learning appears in his *ABC of Action Learning*:

> Action learning is to make useful progress on the treatment of problems/opportunities where no "solution" can possibly exist already because different managers, all honest, experienced, and wise, will advocate different courses of action in accordance with their different value systems, their different past experiences, and their hopes for the future. (1983, p. 28)

Even though a single definition will probably never fully display the complexities of action learning, we believe that definitions are helpful and prompt dialogue for better understanding action learning properties. Here are several current working definitions. Willis has written:

> Action learning is a process of reflecting on one's work and beliefs in a supportive/confrontational environment of one's peers for the purpose of gaining new insights and resolving real business and community problems in real time. (1999)

Yorks, O'Neil, & Marsick define action learning as:

> An approach to working with and developing people that uses work on an actual project or problem as the way to learn. Participants work in small groups to take action to solve their problem and learn how to learn from action. Often a learning coach works with the group in order to help the members learn how to balance their work with the learning from that work. (1999, p. 3)

Marquardt describes action learning as:

> ... both a process and powerful program that involves a small group of people solving real problems while at the same time focusing on what they are learning and how their learning can benefit each group member and the organization as a whole. (1999, p. 4)

Pedler in his *Action Learning in Practice*, says:

> Action learning is a product not of teaching but of tackling problems to which there is no right answer and is about acquiring the ability to ask good questions of oneself, of others, and of situations which lead to an increased ability to tackle problems in the future. (1991, p. 63)

What is common to these four definitions is that real problems become the fulcrum for learning and for action. They also emphasize the reflective component, making meaning out of what is occurring. Further, there is the aspect of mutual collaboration. It is the synergy of the group members, fed by dialogue, that promotes learning. There, too, is the self-dialogue through the process of critical reflection that leads to personal growth.

Goldberg in her book, *The Art of the Question,* addresses the importance of questions versus answers. Certainly the reflective component of action learning is fueled by questions, and

Revans repeatedly makes the point that "fresh" questions are in effect the engine of action learning. The start point is the questioning insight (the Q), not the answers that may have been worked before (the P). Goldberg says this:

> We live in an answer-oriented, fix-it-quick world. In the clamor for answers—sometimes any answer—we often overlook quiet distinctions and fresh perspectives, which could reveal whole worlds of possibilities. Moreover, sometimes the conditioned hunt for answers represents a desperate attachment to 'knowing' and a simultaneous avoidance of any anxiety associated with not knowing, or even appearing not to know. This is ironic as well as unfortunate for often the most bountiful answers are born only after long periods of gestation and living without knowing. (1998, p. 4)

In October 1998, Dilworth, Willis, and Barker met for three days at Oak Island, North Carolina. A central topic of that meeting was characteristics of action learning. The collaborators each independently arrived at what they viewed as the core characteristics (essence) of action learning. They then compared notes and arrived at 24 characteristics of action learning that each could fully endorse. The 24 characteristics are listed below:

1. Confidentiality and mutual trust are necessary.

2. Action learning is egalitarian (equal voice to all).

3. It is a practical approach.

4. You need to consider both programmed knowledge (what has occurred before) and questioning insight, but the starting point is always questioning insight.

5. Action learning operates on the belief that the learning potential is enriched (e.g., intellectually, emotionally) as the unfamiliarity quotient is increased (i.e., unfamiliar problem, unfamiliar setting, unfamiliar colleagues).

6. Learning is given equality or even primacy over problem solution—even though action to resolve the problem is expected.

The Nature of Action Learning

7. There is suspension of judgment pending questioning insight and depth of dialogue (i.e., no predispositions).

8. Diversity of participants enriches the experience (including multicultural).

9. Action learning leads to a broadly encompassing and holistic learning process which impacts individuals and organizations and the interrelationship between them (e.g., organizational change and transformative learning).

10. It is a collaborative learning experience, where those involved learn from and with each other in ways that can promote self-esteem and self-confidence.

11. No set leader is designated. It is rather a case of collective/shared/self-directed leadership.

12. The ideal group size is considered five or six in number to promote effective communication.

13. Action learning involves the deliberate introduction of a consistent learning process that can be used to "unfreeze" dysfunctional organizational cultures and individual mental sets (e.g., being governed by underlying assumptions that are outside the bounds of present-day realities).

14. A facilitator (learning coach) external to the team or group (action learning set) begins the team activity and helps create a framework for the learning process, with varied facilitator involvement thereafter.

15. The inherent emphasis is on reflection-in-action, reflection on reflection-in-action (Schön, 1983, pp. 277–78) and prospective/retrospective action, as in Mumford's Type 2 learning (CCMD Report No. 1, 1999, pp. 3–14).

16. Action learning is built on the belief that the team learns most to the extent it is allowed to select goal(s), project, and the approach(es) to be used to fulfill the shared commitment.

17. Learners are empowered to reframe the goal/problem statement as necessary.

18. Action learning requires support *and* understanding of organizational host/leader/client for maximum benefit to accrue.

19. Participation can be made mandatory in an organization but voluntary participation is the goal.

20. Implementation of a problem diagnosis is ideally achieved through involvement of some or all of those set members who were engaged with problem diagnosis, to complement those who are charged with the implementation and possess the requisite expertise. Therefore, it becomes necessary to create a linking mechanism that allows those charged with implementation to realize ownership in what may have been diagnosed by others.

21. A joint problem that all set members can work on is considered advantageous to one predicated on set members bringing individual work-related issues to the table. Individual projects can lead to unevenness of project complexity and workload between set members, because of such factors as organizational politics and proprietary interests.

22. In cases of conflict resolution, there is a purposeful strategy of avoiding facilitator intervention in favor of the set working through the difficulty and learning from the experience.

23. The set must operate as a cohesive unit with unbroken continuity (presence of all set members at all meetings) for individual and team learning to be fully realized.

24. The problem focus selected is always real, frequently intractable, and never prefabricated as a case study, game, or puzzle.

While most of these characteristics will probably draw wide support among those who practice action learning, not all of them will be agreed upon. For example, there can be wide disparities in interpreting the set advisor (also called learning coach, mentor, or facilitator) role. Throughout the book we will use the term *learning coach*. Some believe that the role of the learning coach is to be omnipresent when sets meet, and rather

The Nature of Action Learning

interventionist in "pushing back," in order to cause learners to stop and reflect on where they are and what is being learned. Others, including Revans, Barker, Dilworth, and Willis, feel strongly that the learning coach should perform in a more stand-off role, recognizing that intervention can hinder rather than promote the learning process. In adult learning theory, the goal is to trust adults as adults, allowing them to make their own meaning. Encouraging independence takes precedence over reinforcing patterns that build dependency. Experiencing uncertainty and having to deal with it without "crutches" or support systems can be a central part of the learning experience for adults.

When you examine the list of 24 characteristics of action learning, it becomes evident that most are not unique to action learning. As stated earlier, action learning is eclectic, drawing from many disciplines and paradigms. What is unique about action learning is the collective mosaic when you bring the 24 characteristics together. No other paradigm to our knowledge does that. Four of the characteristics seem distinctively connected to action learning: number 4 (primacy of questioning insight over programmed knowledge), number 5 (individuals/teams assigned to solve problems with which they have little or no familiarity), number 6 (learning given priority over problem solution) and number 24 (selection of a real problem focus *always*).

THE BASICS OF ACTION LEARNING

The Learning Equation

Revans believes that there are two components of learning, programmed knowledge, which he terms the P factor, and questioning insight or inquiry, which he refers to as the Q factor. It produces the equation $L = P + Q$. Some misinterpret the equation to believe that the P must be attended to first because it is listed first. Revans places the P first because in scientific notation (Revans is a mathematician among other things), the P always comes before Q. Revans's original equation stated that *learning is a function of the combined terms "programmed knowledge" and "questioning insight,"* that is, L= f(P+Q). For those scientfically inclined, a case can be made that it is the *combination* of that which is already known (P) with what is not known (Q) that produces learning, so that P and Q are not sequential outputs of the act, but instead are like a chemical compound in which the elements, once joined, are no longer what they were.

Revans is clear in stating that you need both P and Q, but operationally you always start with Q. His basis for this is that all P is rooted in the past (studies, methods that have been used to solve earlier problems). When you begin with fresh questions (the Q), they can tell you which P you need, whether available P is germane, and whether P exists to cover the situation in which you find yourself.

In 1976, Dilworth was placed in charge of a task force to investigate a major medical problem that had resisted solution for a number of years. Several members of the task force wanted to start by examining earlier studies of the problem, but none of them had led to success. Dilworth advised task force members that the start point would be questions about the issue under study, not the earlier studies. The questions asked conformed to what Revans calls System Alpha, dedicated to exploring the nature of the problem at hand:

1. What is happening?

2. What ought to be happening?

3. What do we need to do to make it happen?

The task force in this case achieved a major breakthrough and gave little attention to the earlier failed attempts.

Others have revised the learning equation. Mumford's variation reflects Q1 + P + Q2 = L = Q3. He is saying in effect that after your introductory Q you turn to P, and then move on to another round of Q. Interplay between P and Q already seems implicit in Revan's formulation.

Leadership in International Management (LIM) speaks of ARL, standing for Action-Reflection-Learning. Again reflection

The Nature of Action Learning

is really a fundamental part of Revans's formulation. In the case of ARL it translates to a model calling for strong learning coach intervention to facilitate the reflection that leads to learning. We consider this a questionable intervention, and one that can interfere with learning rather than foster it.

Marquardt uses the equation $L = P + Q + R$. This is apparently a perceived sequence, and in his book (1999), he indicates that you start with P (p. 29). That breaks sharply with Revans's philosophy, since Revans clearly specifies that the operational start point must be Q. It is Q that expresses the realization that the solution to the problem is *unknown*, or the problem would have been solved already.

Change Versus Learning

Because of the rapidly accelerating rate of change, the rate of learning must similarly accelerate. This is Revans's basic message. To do that requires greater attention to the Q in the learning equation. It runs counter to the way most problem solving is conducted. There is a belief that you need to immerse yourself in the "facts" and study the background before proceeding. Some quality-related programs emphasize "management by fact." Few would argue with management on the basis of facts, but you first need to determine what facts you need. You do that by asking the right questions first (the Q); otherwise you will end up collecting facts that in the end have little relevance to what you are setting out to achieve. Going directly at the problem can appear to be a violation of basic analytical principles. However, there can be much force in starting with our tacit knowledge, drawing on the wellspring of our experiences and those of others. In a sense, it sets you free to probe and explore widely, as opposed to being trapped in the "quicksand of P." It also represents a phenomenological approach. You start with what is there.

As outlined in the three examples that opened this chapter, the learners really had no valid P to turn to. They found themselves on unfamiliar ground; thus, they had to begin with the Q.

Revans also anchors his belief that the Q comes first, and

requires even greater emphasis now, because of the uncertain times in which we live. He describes this need in terms of the relationship between the velocity of change and the velocity of learning. Change is now occurring so rapidly that it can outrun our ability to deal with issues and problems that extend well beyond previous precedent and experience. Revans uses the velocity of information generation and dissemination as one index to a rapidly accelerating rate of change. He points out that when change outruns the ability to adapt, organizations (and for that matter, individuals), can find themselves in a dangerous state. What needs to occur is a better alignment between the rate of learning and the rate of change. In Figure 1.1, the range of organizational adaptability to rate of change has been added to Revans's concept of the parallel velocities of physical travel and knowledge travel. Some organizations and individuals always seem to be ahead of the velocity of change in terms of learning, but many lag far behind (below the curves shown).

The Four Squares of Action Learning

Revans believes that there are two kinds of problems we end up confronting in life, and two types of settings in which we encounter them. They are either familiar or unfamiliar. To that, we add *colleagues*, for they can either be familiar or unfamiliar as well. Figure 1.2 is the basic diagram that Revans uses, to which we have added some of our own examples:

Our usual placement in this "four-square" diagram is in quadrant A, where we find ourselves in the surroundings of our own workplace dealing with familiar problems. We turn to the P instinctively in this situation. How did we deal with the issue last month, last week, yesterday? Do we have a standard operating procedure we can turn to?

Quadrant D is another matter. Here we are on unfamiliar ground and facing something we have not seen before, or at least know very little about. Compounding matters, we may find ourselves in a team of people we do not know or have never worked with previously. This unfamiliar-unfamiliar setting and prob-

The Nature of Action Learning

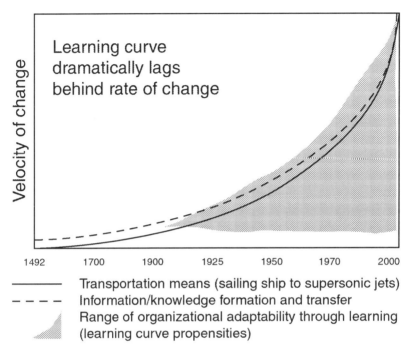

Figure 1.1 Rate of Change Versus Rate of Learning (After R. W. Revans, Seminar at Virginia Commonwealth University, February 1994)

lem (and even colleagues) according to Revans, is where the largest learning yields are likely to be realized. He has also identified it with what is necessary to build learning organizations.

Revans's study of the coal mines falls in quadrant A. He was dealing with natural teams of miners, practicing their trade where they were accustomed to practice it, at the coalface. Action learning can be effective in quadrant A. It is in quadrant A where you customarily find the best examples of quality circles.

Revans's Hospital Intercommunication Study (HIC) usually fell in quadrant B. Although the setting may have resembled their normal work environment, learners went to a different hospital. While the problem might typically fall in the realm of the familiar, it could just as easily fall in the area of unfamiliarity if the set found itself dealing with something outside their

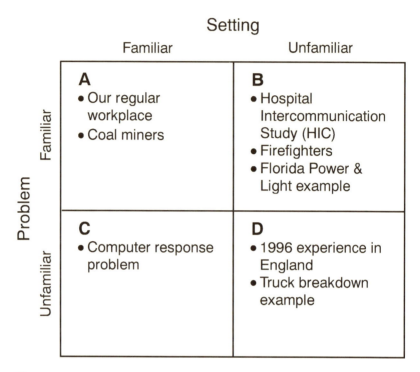

Figure 2.1 Action Learning in Contexts

normal area of expertise, such as those from the pediatrics area looking at a problem occurring in cardiology. In any case, the problem being dealt with was in a different hospital context and culture, and that could create a problem texture somewhat removed from their past experience. In 1996, we were involved with an action learning program related to the consolidation of two major hospitals in the Manchester area of England. The two cultures could not have been more different even though only a few miles apart.

Firefighters find themselves in an unfamiliar setting, but usually dealing with problems that they have seen before and have been trained to confront. This is an example of quadrant B.

The computer response problem example provided earlier falls in quadrant C. The management interns were operating in an organization they knew relatively well, but the problem did not fit with their background, training, or experience. They also were working with colleagues whom they barely knew. The truck problem example fits quadrant D. The soldiers were unfamiliar with the problem being dealt with, and being broken down on a remote road was not where they normally operated. On the other hand, they seemed to know each other well, and through synergy, were able to capitalize on their collective strengths.

In 1996 we led an action learning experience in England, involving participants from the United States, Canada, and Australia. The vast majority of those participating (28 of 31) had no experience with the problem being addressed by their action learning sets (health care related). None had been to this locale before, and few knew each other. This is another quadrant D example.

Action Versus Reflection

In action learning, it is the reflective component, critically examining one's assumptions in relation to what is occurring, that pushes the learning envelope. Action must be balanced by reflection. In actual practice, this is a very difficult balance to achieve. In the U.S. culture, there is almost an unquenchable thirst to drive after the problem to the exclusion of everything else. Stopping to reflect can seem like a diversion, a pointless delay. If you recommend that an interval be created to allow some reflective time, individually and by the group, it can be sharply resisted.

There is no greater challenge in action learning than striking the balance between action and reflection. But it does not require a learning coach as a "policeman" to ensure that it occurs. It requires that learners understand the process and reasons for it coupled with selective and occasional coaching by the learning coach to reinforce the need for reflection. Use of learning logs and other techniques can also promote critical reflection.

As action learners come to recognize the importance of the reflective component and how it can actually fuel arrival at a solution, they tend to welcome it. The quality of the critical reflection can also be the key to individual participant growth.

One dynamic that can promote reflection is the diversity of the set/team composition. It brings a variety of perspectives into play and this can help induce reflection. We use the Honey-Mumford Learning Style Questionnaire (LSQ) as one means of helping to create the balance between action and reflection. For example, if a team of six people has four or five strong to very strong activists, it can literally shut down the reflective inclinations. Similarly, an excessive number of strong reflectors in a team can curtail action. The intent is not to seek some form of perfect balance. That would assign too high a value to the ability of the LSQ, or any instrument, to precisely discern learning style differences. The intent is rather to balance the properties to the extent possible. The LSQ results can open up important dialogue. Direct knowledge of the participants is also a prime reference point in arriving at a mix of personalities that can help achieve an action-reflection balance.

Egalitarian Nature of Action Learning

It is often wise to assign people to an action learning set who are roughly on a par with each other in terms of level of experience and age. On the other hand, there are examples of mixing status levels rather broadly (e.g., an entry level worker in a set with a corporate vice president). The latter approach can help open up dialogue across boundaries and levels in an organization. It has been used in recent years to promote dialogue around "learning maps" and bring all employees to a shared vision, without regard to status or time with the organization. In some national cultures, it can be unnatural and problematic to mix status levels in a set (for example, an Asian culture).

Whether drawn from a similar or different organizational level, it is important that all have equivalent status within the

The Nature of Action Learning 23

team. Leaders are not designated and while an action learning set will commonly divide up some of the responsibilities, the set does not operate with a designated leader. Quite often, leadership responsibility is broadly shared or rotated and this often occurs naturally depending upon the issue being addressed. In 1996, an action learning participant familiar to one of us ended up besieged with questions from non-action learning participants on who was leading her team. In frustration, she finally said: "We all are leaders!" Action learning sets are really akin to self-directed work teams in terms of their internal leadership structure. You can watch an effective action learning set operate and be unable to detect the primacy of any one set member in the process.

The egalitarian nature of action learning can run crossgrain to organizational culture. There can be some set members, from time to time, who will try to exert authority within an action learning set, but that will usually be quickly countered by other team members. In 1996, in England, in an action learning experience that we shared, one participant attempted to take over a set as it began its daily meeting. The other members picked up their chairs and turned their backs to her, communicating that they found her behavior unacceptable. In another incident, a participant similarly started to outline the day's activities without prior coordination. Another participant called an immediate halt to the proceedings. After almost three hours of honest and open dialogue, the errant participant understood never to violate group norms again. In yet another example, a set member presented for the set without prior coordination of fellow set members. After the session, set members told their colleague never to do that again!

At the beginning of an action learning experience, set members are asked to develop collectively the rules that will govern their behavior. Equality of voice is an important part of such conventions; respect for one another is usually another. However, there can also be times when set members will not confront dysfunctional behavior, believing that confrontation will only exacerbate the problem. In such cases the situation can worsen and lead to even greater problems. The best rule of thumb is to address the issue promptly within the action learning set. Problems with group dynamics if left unattended can severely impact the learning experience.

Facilitation of Action Learning

The facilitation of action learning sets has received some address already as part of the discussion of the characteristics of action learning earlier in this chapter. The nature of facilitation is arguably the most controversial aspect of action learning. Revans believes that less facilitation of action learning sets is better than more. He views adults as their own best facilitators. Elsewhere, views on facilitation, the set advisement role, or learning coach cover a continuum from almost none to virtually constant presence when the set is in session. There are interesting arguments given by those who endorse having a set advisor constantly present. One well-known authority on action learning says: "How would I know what is going on if I am not there?" No amount of argument will usually dissuade people from holding to that point of view. We believe in very selective involvement with the set by those external to it. From the standpoint of group dynamics, a learning coach is not a benign presence when an action learning set is in session. They are, whether they view themselves as such or not, perceived to be people of authority and influence. Therefore, their presence will have an influence on group dynamics.

We certainly agree that maturity of the learners can influence the amount of coaching/facilitation that is appropriate. For example, dealing with teenagers can inherently require more involvement. On the other hand, we can think of examples where this simply did not hold true. An especially meaningful example relates to an action learning set of last chance offenders in the criminal justice system of Virginia. All were on parole. Each of the six participants had violated parole twice. This was literally their last chance before being returned to prison to serve out their full sentences. The expectation was that because of their perceived immaturity, they would need a learning coach to constantly guide them. That did not prove out. After the first

10 minutes of their first meeting together, they took charge of their own learning and became almost oblivious to the presence of the learning coach. One of the participants successfully changed his pattern of behavior during this action learning program, met his parole requirements, and ended up working for the State of Virginia in helping other last chance offenders.

The best formula, in our view, is to use a learning coach up front to jump-start the action learning process. Then, it should be a case of fading back and not attending set meetings unless invited to do so. This can be referred to as the principle of "invitation only." There are two forms of "invitation only" evident in action learning programs. Our formulation involves no entry of a set by the learning coach unless invited or based on prearrangement. That is the approach we favor. Other practitioners use "invitation only" in the sense that the learning coach is in the room but will only intervene in the set business by invitation. That is quite different and, as already mentioned, the mere presence of a learning coach in the room constitutes an intervention. That is well documented in group dynamics.

When learning coaches enter and exit a set in an interruptive manner, and intervene when present, special problems can be created. It can be extremely frustrating to members of a set. We have seen learning coaches asked to leave a set by its members, when they considered the interruptions of the learning coach to be objectionable. In one instance a learning coach entered a set area, and interrupted the conversation to ask if he could provide any assistance. One of the set members barked, "Yes, you can leave!" We know of one case when the learning coach was told to leave and never to return. Regarding such "expert" interruptions, Weisbord has this to say: "The expert arrives in the middle of somebody else's movie and leaves before the movie ends" (1987, p. 190).

LINKS TO ADULT EDUCATION AND HRD

Probably no one has defined adult education better than Eduard Lindeman, who said in his book, *The Meaning of Adult Education:*

> ... education is life—not a mere preparation for an unknown kind of future living. Consequently all static concepts of education which relegate the learning process to the period of youth are abandoned. (1926, republished in 1961, p. 4)

Lindeman viewed learning as coterminous with life, a philosophy that dovetails closely with the real-life problem solving of action learning. He was also the first to use the term *andragogy* in the United States (1926), a term later popularized by Malcolm Knowles. "The term (andragogik) was first coined ... by the German grammar school teacher, Alexander Knapp, in 1833" (Knowles, 1990, p. 52). The term *andragogy* represents a unified theory of adult learning, and is distinguished from the theory of youth learning, pedagogy (p. 51). The term *pedagogy*, on the other hand, " ... is derived from the Greek word, meaning 'child' (the same stem from which pediatrics comes)" (p. 54).

Knowles went on to describe why the andragogical model is different from the pedagogical model. He found five principal differences. They are:

1. The need to know. Adults need to know why they need to learn something before undertaking to learn it.

2. The learners' concept. Adults have a self-concept of being responsible for their own decisions, for their own lives.

3. The role of learners' experience. Adults come into an educational activity with both a greater volume and a different quality of experience from youths.

4. Readiness to learn. Adults become ready to learn those things they need to know and be able to do in order to cope effectively with their real-life situations.

5. Orientation to learning. In contrast to children's and youth's subject-oriented orientation to learning, adults are life-centered or task-centered (or problem-centered) in their orientation to learning (pp. 57–61).

What is significant is that the pedagogical model turns out to be the way many university and college classrooms organize the learning experience. It can be a didactic, one-way means of communication, with adult students expected to learn by taking lecture notes. It is not necessarily a learner-centered environment with adults allowed to participate in agenda setting. Instruction can be viewed by learners as irrelevant to the life experiences, and learner readiness to learn can be low.

Action learning fits well with the andragogical principles enumerated by Knowles. Learner readiness flows out of the perceived relevance and meaningfulness of the experience. Participants are both empowered and enabled to determine learning strategies that work best for them. This is key because adults have different learning styles, and different motivational factors can be at work. Action learning affords the necessary flexibility, allowing the learners to shape and customize the learning experience. We have found that participants in an action learning experience, when asked what stands out for them, will say something along the lines of "I felt free to learn."

Jack Mezirow, Professor Emeritus at Columbia University, Teachers College, a world-renowned adult educator, has written extensively about transformational learning. We will address this more fully in Chapter 7. Based on dozens of action learning experiences over the years, we see a definite link between action learning and transformational learning. A significant number of action learning participants have, in reflective essays written after the experience, reported a sense of being transformed.

In Mezirow's writings, we find specific connections between transformative learning, action learning, and the rudiments of adult education as outlined by Lindeman, Knowles, and others. You can see the link between andragogical principles and transformative learning when Mezirow says "Our actions toward things are based on the meaning that the things have for us." He also says, and you get a clear tie-in with action learning: "conception determines perception, and we can only know reality by acting on it" (1991, p. xiv).

We have discussed the impact of having individuals work in settings with people and on problems that are unfamiliar to them. This can be unsettling and disorienting, and can cause people to think outside the parameters of the assumptions (which can be subconscious) that govern their actions. This can lead to a rethinking of who we are and what controls our thought processes. Such gains can occur through the reflection component of action learning. Mezirow adds:

> Reflective learning involves assessment or reassessment of assumptions. Reflective learning becomes transformative whenever assumptions or premises are found to be distorting, inauthentic, or otherwise invalid. (1991, p. 6)

In recent years, human resource development has come to align itself more tightly with adult education principles, including job announcements that emphasize knowledge of adult learning principles. Leonard Nadler, who coined the term *human resource development (HRD)* in the 1960s, considers HRD to be adult education in organizations. That is not necessarily what has been true. The HR emphasis in companies has often had a scope that stopped short of anything beyond formal training. There can be a mesmerization with curriculum development and design. Gilley and Maycunich state: "When HRD professionals believe that the business of HRD is to deliver *training for training's sake*, all the energy is directed toward the number of training courses they deliver and the number of employees they train" (1998, p. 1). The andragogical principles of Lindeman and Knowles are not always evident in the practice of human resource development. That is now changing, and action learning is helping to create this change.

HOW ACTION LEARNING FITS WITH THE CHALLENGES NOW CONFRONTING ORGANIZATIONS

Action learning is increasingly seen as a learning strategy of choice, in some cases with a clear intent to trigger cultural transformation in the organization. General Electric (GE) has been an advocate of action learning since the mid-1980s, and it has played a role in their "work-out" technology, a process that allows employees to become directly involved with key problem-solving challenges and the presentation of recommendations to top-level managers for decision.

The list of companies using action learning has become quite extensive. A partial list of organizations that are now using or have used action learning includes Whirlpool, Corning, GTE Corporation, Ameritech, Federal Deposit Insurance Corporation (FDIC), Conoco-Houston, Bristol-Myers Squibb, Union Carbide, Public Electric and Gas (New Jersey), Ford, and Honda.

It would be misleading, however, to think of action learning as applicable only or perhaps even mainly to the corporate environment. A number of universities are using or have used programs centered on action learning. In the United States, they include Virginia Commonwealth University, Georgia State University, George Washington University, Florida Atlantic University, University of Texas at Austin, George Mason University, Eastern Connecticut University, and Rice University. Abroad, a notable program is located at the Revans Institute for Action Learning and Research at the University of Salford, in England. Other programs in different forms can be found around the world, including developing countries.

Why is action learning receiving so much attention? It fits with the times, especially in terms of the rapid changes taking place. Marquardt (1999, p. 5) attributes the surge of interest to the fact that action learning can be applied simultaneously to the five most important needs facing organizations (including nonprofit organizations) today:

1. Problem solving

2. Organizational learning

3. Team building

4. Leadership development

5. Professional growth and career development

To Marquardt's list we would add learning to learn, adaptability to change, and self-efficacy raising. Learning to learn is frequently listed by organizations as a pressing need and precursor to other forms of learning programs. It seems to naturally occur in an action learning experience. The intensity of an action learning experience also causes the learners to adapt very quickly. In dealing with problem solving in relation to major issues that are unfolding, events can be highly unpredictable and fast paced. In too many cases, organizations have become deeply demoralized as a result of abrupt and frequent restructuring, some of it poorly conceived and communicated. They are waiting for the other shoe to fall. Properly employed, action learning can begin to rebuild the trust necessary for effective corporate education programs and build employee self-confidence.

One of the most significant developments in the United States has been the advent of corporate universities, now totaling over 1,000 and expected to grow to 2,000 or more within 10 years. Meister has written extensively on the emerging phenomenon. Her model for creating a corporate university is widely employed. She says this about action learning:

> Today the venue is most likely to be the workplace, and rather than learning the five or seven steps to creative thinking, managers are now involved in action learning and computer simulations where they examine business strategies and recommend real-time solutions. Action learning is "training" that takes the form of an actual business problem for teams of learners to solve together. (1998, p. 110)

Meister cites Kodak as a company that is using action learning to encourage creative thinking rather than teaching creativity in a static course (p. 111). Many other companies have found their way to a similar orientation. However, it is not widely talked about. Strategies like action learning, when they produce competitive advantage, can be as closely guarded as the recipes for the Campbell soups. This can make it difficult to fully gauge what is happening in corporations with regard to action learning. One thing is apparent though. Action learning is catching on rapidly, and it is seen as an approach that can deliver significant results.

Action learning is also extremely compatible with the em-

The Nature of Action Learning

phasis on organizational learning, creating learning organizations, continuous learning, and lifelong learning. Action learning can be used as a means of better integrating an enterprise. This can be done by creating action learning sets that draw their membership from across a company, a government agency, or a nonprofit organization. The outcome can be an opening up of communication channels, a deepening of employee networks cross-functionally, and better employee understanding of overall programs and vision. This certainly dovetails with GE's interest in building a "boundaryless company."

SUMMARY

Action learning comes in many garden varieties. It is eclectic, drawing from many disciplines. At the same time it has some distinctive features about it that make it unique. One example is its encouragement of problem solving that places learners outside of their expertise. Its egalitarian nature can also break sharply with the command and control, hierarchical authority structures still found in a number of organizations. As will be pointed out later in the book, it can be necessary to prepare the organizational culture for the introduction of action learning, as well as having top management understanding and support.

Action learning is increasingly becoming a learning strategy of choice because of its fit with the changing dynamics of our time. At present, it is much more prevalent in the business sector than it is in academe. However, even this is now beginning to change, even though the culture of academic institutions tends to be much more resistant to incorporation of action learning approaches.

Figure 1.3 shows the linkage of action learning to adult education and other learning methods now being emphasized. The figure represents the cascading effect as one action learning process leads to another and yet another. The starting point is fresh questions, best induced when the learner is confronted with the unfamiliar. Long-held assumptions can prove dysfunctional to the learner operating in an unfamiliar, even disorient-

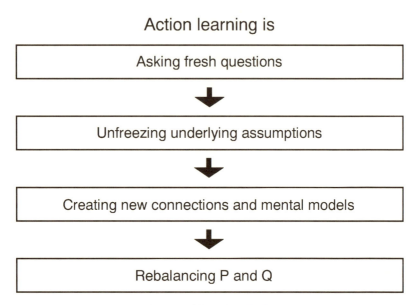

Figure 1.3 Action Learning in a Nutshell

ing environment. Action learning may have specified time frames, but like all learning, it percolates through whatever boundaries may be set.

When you are out of your customary comfort zone, you have reason to examine the existing assumptions critically. You can end up "unfreezing" assumptions and searching for new ones. This, in turn, can produce new mental models. Out of the process comes an assessment of P, looking at it in the bright light of reality. Is it really relevant, or is it riddled with inconsistencies and insights better suited for an earlier time? Since you need P, how will you now close the gaps in P exposed through questioning insight Q? You may end up needing to create new P, gathering facts that might have previously appeared to have limited value, or collecting data that has never been captured before.

CHAPTER 2

Action Learning in Various Contexts

It is often difficult to identify the truly fundamental assumptions that are shaping one's thoughts and actions. But it is important to do so, to avoid being dominated by them.... What are the dominant assumptions and beliefs that shape how you think about your organizations? Try and document them.
— Gareth Morgan (1989, p. 28)

We depend on the minds of others, on their being healthy and well-intentioned.... Every institution should be open to judgements about the mentalities they tend to create, whether they leave those who come into contact with them stronger or weaker, more able to bear responsibilities or less so, ethically fluent or ethically stunted.
— Geoff Mulgan (1997, p. 123)

Social and philosophical commitments that fostered the development of a particular field at one period of time have sometimes hampered it at another ...
— Thomas S. Kuhn (1977, p. 33)

Using action learning and encouraging others to do so lead us often to a favorite saying: "No two action learning experiences and no two action learning sets are ever alike." The process and outcomes will vary according to who is in the set, what the set is working on, and in what context the work and learning are occurring. This is no cause for alarm. Predictability is not what we are after. Action learning thrives, creates, and recreates on a steady diet of variety.

We offer this chapter as a here-and-now example of the fruitful digressions that occur in action learning. When we pause and review whatever we have been discussing, probing deeper into our own uncertainties, new ideas tend to surface in illuminating the problem at hand. The following discussion is meant to draw you directly into the heart of the reflective process (that is, the source of the Gamma personal and organizational growth that Revans talks about).

Without you to pause and reflect with us, this chapter will fall short of its mark. Action learning requires your involvement, because you—along with us—are at once the learners and the action takers. The Gamma system, which depends on reflection to fuel it, isn't anything alien to you. Even if the term itself may not be one we commonly use, every one of us naturally stops from time to time in the midst of what we are doing "to think about what we are thinking about." We try to figure out what our actions and thoughts mean, why we should care, and what we ought to do next. It is simply that action learning in its group form raises the power of this human reflective capability exponentially. It gives us comrades enjoined to share and help illuminate our thinking-learning-doing paths.

There are counterforces. Our formal educational experiences, vital and necessary as they are, have also taught us to trust neatly organized bodies of knowledge more than we trust the chaotic inquiry processes that produced the knowledge in the first place. Action learning reverses that order. It forces us to look at the "mental sets," the assumptions, the biases, the habits of mind, the unseen boundaries we have set against our own further learning. The same factors bind not only the things we can think, but also the things we believe we can do.

In the discussion that follows, come with us and explore the reservations people have expressed about using action learning in their own particular settings. This demands some archival digging, then some dusting off of the findings to see what habits of thought may lie beneath these reservations. Over and over, we hear the claim that "It may be all right for your organization, but it won't work *here*." We ask ourselves: Why is it that action learning, apparently so human and so natural, raises such skepticism?

To find out, we start with the contexts, that is, the potential practice settings, and then work our way down through layers of thought patterns and beliefs that seem to circulate and become embedded in these contexts. Remember that this is reflection time, and that we are asking you to reflect with us and give us feedback. We mean this literally. Talk back to us and give us the benefit of your own perspectives. The asynchronous nature of our communication—book to e-mail, letter, or phone call—should not stop you, because perspective sharing is continually cited as one of the most valued outcomes of action learning. We would hate to be among those who miss out on this kind of exchange.

Remember also that reflection, like every other part of action learning, uses both the P of programmed knowledge and the Q of our curiosity and questioning capacity. Because reflection leans heavily toward Q, further inquiry may gradually or even suddenly modify statements we are making with great conviction now.

APPLICATION DOMAINS AND SPECIFIC CONTEXTS

Selected practice environments are grouped in Figure 2.1 for convenience of discussion, but there is certainly cross-hatching of interests across groups. The first column clusters the practice settings by domain. The second column indicates specific contexts (implying our respective practitioner realms or "comfort zones") that are environments in which action learning has either already found a home, or might profitably do so. The chart is representative, rather than exhaustive. In at least one and probably more than one of the 16 adult learning, HRD, and international development arenas, most of you will be able to find a conceptual or organizational fit for yourselves. We know of action learning projects in each of the domains and in a ma-

Possible Contexts for Action Learning

Domain	Specific Context
Academic Settings	1 Higher education (general)
	2 Adult education and HRD professional programs
	3 Community colleges
	4 Adult education outside academe (e.g., adult basic education)
Private Sector Businesses and Services	5 Major private companies
	6 Corporate universities
	7 New economy businesses
	8 Small businesses and nonprofits
Governments	9 Federal
	10 State
	11 County and municipal
World	12 International organizations (e.g., UN, World Bank, World Health Organization)
	13 Nongovernment organizations (NGOs) (e.g., Doctors Without Borders, International Red Cross)
System Changers	14 Organization development (OD)
	15 Chief learning officer (CLO)
	16 Other HRD practitioners

Figure 2.1 Action Learning in Contexts

jority but not all of the specific contexts. There is plenty of room for expansion into other areas of work and life beyond those identified here.

We acknowledge that there is overlap among the designated environments and the practitioners (system changers) who serve them, but nevertheless it seems helpful to imagine these as 16 different settings with driving forces and constraints that belong to each. In Chapter 6 we will describe how we can work operationally with or against the forces that help or hinder the use of action learning in specific contexts.

If you have not been able to envision yourselves working in any of the listed environments, you may well find creative applications of your own—as did an Australian nun who discovered that engaging homeless people in action learning helped them acquire the means to change their status. Participants in other places not included in the 16 settings have found opportunities to induce positive effects very close at hand, influencing family dynamics and remodeling their own motivations through encounters with action learning. It seems that even programs of very short duration provide stimulus for new insights and behaviors.

Context-Fed Biases

Different kinds of practice settings have different kinds of assumptions and biases to work through before a clear picture of potential applications of action learning begins to emerge. We can make educated guesses, but find it difficult to specify in advance for any organization which kinds of applications may ultimately work and which may not. That will depend on the organization, the type and strength of the biases and assumptions prevailing there, the commitment to learning and trial, and the nature and degree of investment in the problem to be addressed.

We know that biases easily grow deep roots and are difficult to dislodge. They seem, like Atlas, to "hold up the world" as we know it. Unfortunately, they also tend to roll over into "law-like" assumptions that can initially stand in the way of our gaining either a panoramic or a close-up view of action learning. What we assume keeps us from seeing what is actually there. As Morgan says, "Our ways of seeing are shaped by numerous hidden forces that make reality real in a culturally specific way" (1989, p. 21).

When we analyze the questions people typically raise about the usefulness of action learning, we see that they begin to make comparisons of this new possibility with whatever they already know about. Then the biases begin to boil up out of the context.

Here are a few examples: "What is it that you teach? How will we know what people have learned? How can action learning as you describe it ever hope to compete with e-learning in this day and age? Isn't good leadership always the key to any problem-solving activity? In these examples, there are biases you will recognize, and may even subscribe to. Each question serves to illustrate mind sets currently in force regarding each of these aspects of learning: (1) curriculum dominance, (2) "learning guarantees," (3) "learning on the fly" (technology-driven), and (4) leader control of learning.

We turn now to the four common assumptions that we believe are the unrecognized basis for expressions of reservations about action learning. It is hard to fit action learning into a world squared by these assumptions, as you will see.

FOUR COMMON ASSUMPTIONS

Assumption 1. Learning and Curriculum Are Indivisible.

Because people are products of educational systems, one of the most common assumptions is that when learning is to be done, then also there is an identifiable content to be learned and a curriculum to be planned. Even if the participants in the learning are to build the curriculum themselves, there is an automatic expectation that there will be one. It is taken for granted that "subject matter" drives the idea of learning, and that the first questions to ask will be content, instructional design, and delivery questions.

The curriculum, "course-of-study" mindset is so common across all kinds of organizations that it can hold action learning hostage from the very beginning. If one has the traditional understanding that learning and curriculum are joined at the hip, then it is ever so hard to see how action learning, which isn't curriculum based, can be such a powerful learning tool. According to Weinstein (1995), "In a 'classic' action learning program, there is no taught element" (p. 41). This can be a mystifying proposition; the very thought of learning in an action learning context where nothing is being "taught" raises issues of credibility to those who are teachers or trainers. It affects other domains as well, for all are touched in some way by the habit of thinking that people learn best by being skillfully taught.

A major reason why curriculum becomes a moot issue in action learning is that what needs to be learned can seldom be predicted in a deliberately real-world, real-time chase-down of a real, stubborn problem. The problem, viewed from at least a half dozen different angles if there are that number of people in an action learning set, gets peeled like a layered onion, and in the process may begin to look like something very different from what was originally supposed. Reliance on process naturally takes precedence; the unfolding insights and deepening inquiry of action learning draw their force *from set members, what they already know, and what they are giving attention to*. Their concentration is on tackling the problem, trying to understand what happens behind the problem and how people are affected by it. A preplanned curriculum would be brushed aside early in set deliberations, as participants scramble for on-site information and recover forgotten facts and feelings from themselves and from the set environment.

An example of this sidelining of subject matter "content" occurred in a large oil company, where a "lending library" was provided for each action learning set. Some individuals took out books or videos and returned them read, half-read, or unread, but whatever the case, it was clear by the third meeting that the immediacy of the problems they were struggling with overrode the unfocused search for P. This is further evidence for our assertion that the P already present in the adult set is more than sufficient to justify beginning action learning with Q, the quest for fresh questions to ask and answer.

Assumption 2. Accountability for Learning Means Offering "Learning Guarantees."

Another common assumption is that there must be "learning guarantees" in order for any learning initiative to be judged worthwhile. In action learning, this is like saying that a whole new way of looking at the world is inconsequential unless it directly, immediately, and measurably affects the bottom line. The blinders in place here are the biases toward instrumental learning, as if the only learning that can have economic value is to "get that job in the first place," or to "do the existing job better than others might." While instrumental learning has its valued place even in action learning, it is a limiting concept, tough to get beyond in order to explain the infinitely more comprehensive range of action learning benefits that flourish if allowed to emerge. Action learning cannot be described by using simple ideas of skill accrual.

Assumption 3. "Learning on the Fly" Is a Viable Substitute for Group Processing of Learning.

The rise of technology-based learning has led to a widely held assumption that "learning on the fly" is not only possible, but utterly desirable. Learning is a thing to be grabbed off the screen, snatched in passing, almost as if it were an airport food phenomenon. It is characteristic of this bias that learning is perceived as "just in time" to get someone to a specific knowledge destination, either a destination of the learner's own choice or a destination mandated by a sponsoring organization. It is essentially a consumer phenomenon that, although it may not ignore the need to reflect on what is learned, certainly places a higher priority on speed to the learning source, speed through the packaged content, and speed to application. It is a technical response to the problem of the rate of change. Again, however, a curriculum bias is evident even though what is to be learned may be delivered in incisive, creative, and compelling ways. There is a "content" to be delivered, even if it no longer requires a classroom.

The face-to-face requirement of action learning means that although set members may independently make use of any online or archived information that they can unearth, very quickly they must sit down together, talk over what they have found, reflect on its importance, and decide collectively what is or is not relevant to the problem at hand.

Assumption 4. Leaders of Learning Events and Processes Are by Definition on the Control Side of What Can or Should Happen.

Still another indelible bias that makes it difficult to show how action learning is different from other kinds of learning programs is the bias toward leader control. Having a management mindset means that to manage well, one must control outcomes and by inference, the processes by which outcomes are achieved. At the very least, control-oriented leaders believe they must personally clear away organizational messes and set definite goals for the learning and action of subordinates.

Acceptance of the responsibility to control is a mindset shared by classroom teachers and administrators. The "teacher-centered" classroom may have migrated toward the "resource-rich" classroom, but the idea of leader preplanning and control of what learners will study and how they will be engaged has lost little ground. Even if committed to the creation of learner-centered projects, faculty and administrators find themselves bowing to the control bias prevailing in their institutions, often compromising their original intentions.

The leader as facilitator of learning embodies the same bias. As noted earlier, facilitator or learning coach styles seem to arrange themselves on a continuum between extremes of strong control and on-call backup support for small group endeavors. Those who view facilitation as orchestration may take their cues from the behavior of symphony conductors, well known for their skill and power in eliciting from the performers the conductor's own visions of what a composer has to say. Performers themselves interpret the way the conductor wants them to interpret.

Those who view the facilitator's role as nondirective and who consider the group perfectly capable of determining its own course of action run the risk of being found nonessential once the learning process has been set in motion. In between these extremes, action learning seems to take on a life of its own, neither requesting nor wanting facilitation.

There are two major reasons why the bias toward leader control needs to be looked at seriously before undertaking an action learning project. The first is that if leader control is a hidebound expectation in an organization, it will certainly take courage and perhaps even a bit of subversive strategizing to find acceptance for the democratization that action learning encourages. The second reason this bias needs attention is that a learning coach/facilitator's own vision of what will or should happen may itself stand as a barrier to adult learning and problem working. Learning coach biases and preferences for outcomes as well as for high or low structure really matter. Furthermore, by their own admission some facilitators hope that action learning will be an opening gambit for the later sale of content-oriented workshops and courses (Inglis, 1994, p. 201).

Once again, the bias toward curriculum (topic-organized content) resurfaces, this time both as the expectation of organizations and as the expectation of the service provider or consultant. This is a strong part of the justification for learning-leader control. It is assumed that the leader will know or be able to ferret out what the learners need to know and furnish their minds accordingly.

ASSUMPTIONS LINKED TO "CORRIGIBLE HANDICAPS"

Before we turn to comments on mindsets to watch for as we look at potential sites for action learning—mindsets that will be dead giveaways of the presence of the four assumptions —we refer to what Revans has to say about limiting conditions that influence action learning. The work we cite is itself an action learning handbook, and it helps to explain why we get sandbagged by common assumptions and mindsets and find it so difficult to overcome them.

In *ABC of Action Learning*, Revans has listed four "corrigible handicaps" that influence managerial work, and by implication, any work that involves "the typical tasks of deciding what needs to be done in conditions of risk and confusion." Far from being daunted by these handicaps, Revans calls them "corrigible," that is, correctable by openly addressing their presence in persons and environments. The handicaps are human tendencies toward the following:

1. "the idolization of perceived past experience"

2. "the charismatic influences of successful (other) managers [leaders]"

3. "the impulsion to instant activity"

4. "the belittlement of subordinates" (p. 5, first printing; p. 39, 1983 edition with word "corrigible" omitted)

While Revans refers specifically to the myopia of individual managers, the handicaps to learning that he names also seem characteristic of whole organizations caught up in their own histories. We apply the list in a collective sense and consider it a penetrating insight into barriers to problem solving in organizations. It serves almost equally well as a macro view of potential barriers to the adoption and implementation of action learning programs. While all four of the handicaps ring true in this new application, it is the idolizing of perceived past experience and the impulse to instant activity that may stand most in the way of promoting action learning in people and organizations. The first handicap uncritically turns the eyes of potential learners backward to what they have already learned, and the third insists that there is simply no time at all for people to learn before they are forced to act.

Entrenched, programmed knowledge and the inability to break away from it are keys in each case. No room is left for questioning old premises or embarking on groundbreaking inquiry. Restating the Revans handicaps this baldly makes it seem as if no organization could sensibly harbor them, yet they remain potent and ubiquitous.

A chief requirement for action learning is the capacity to unlearn, to lay aside habits of thought that are deeply ingrained, familiar, and comfortable. Such habits inform and predispose everything we do. There are efficiencies gained, for it is habit of thought that prevents us from having to reinvent the wheel each time a wheel is needed. On the downside, we are often efficiently prevented from realizing that the wheel available does not really bear the weight of today's problem. Thus habitual thought patterns compromise effectiveness, turning what we have already carefully figured out and think we can depend on into a series of absolutes that bar further reflection. This has already been noted in Chapter 1, but the potency of reliance on what has gone before, that is, the idolization of past experience, cannot be overemphasized.

MINDSETS TO WATCH FOR

Characteristic habits of thought, lodged in education and experience, live in each person and in each organizational setting although there may be varying levels of awareness that this is so. There are also varying degrees of fixation with these thought habits, as well as ways to dismiss them as useless vestiges of "old paradigms." Those who introduce the concepts and practices of action learning in any setting need first to anticipate or investigate what habitual thought patterns are in play in that setting, how entrenched they are, and how these may influence adoption and outcomes.

Fixed thoughts are like fixed incomes; in times of crisis there is little elasticity. As the price of thinking in fixed ways goes up in organizations striving to stretch and cover more and more bases with the same resources, threadbare spots begin to show up with increasing regularity. The poverty of habitual thinking starts to hurt. Many organizations have come to see the bare spots very clearly, know patching isn't working, but are at a loss to know what to do next. It is these organizations that may be most likely to try action learning.

It is simplistic to say that "people resist change," as if the problem were rooted in individual stubbornness or longing to hang on to the past. The truth is that people who mount change efforts run smack up against the habits of thought, mental sets, disciplinary boundaries, field orientations, and worldviews that are a deliberate legacy of discipline-organized educational systems. Each discipline claims exclusive rights to its own body of knowledge, with defining habits of thought attached to the body. Together, these slowly grow "the expert" in any given field and close off access to non-expert points of view.

Compounding this is not only the fact that organizations tend to have varying mixes of the disciplines, but also that each organization has dominant traditions and expectations that keep surfacing no matter how eager its leaders may be to sign the organization up for change. Clearly it is a thick stew of disciplinary points of view, experiential biases, assumptions, traditions, and habits of thought that can prevail against the spontaneity of action learning if we do not prepare the way for its acceptance.

A next step in our preparation for action learning trials may be to link the limiting assumptions clearly to the domains of practice of most concern to each of us. After a brief recapping of the similarity relations between the assumptions and Revans's "handicaps," we develop hypotheses about relative strengths and distributions of the assumptions across all five of the domains. This should help us not only to view potential barriers to action learning in context, but also to discover possible ways to soften the influence of these barriers.

Recap of the Four Common Assumptions

Individually, the assumptions may be presumed to receive varying degrees of emphasis across the five application domains, even though they are likely to be present in greater or lesser strength in all. It should be abundantly clear by now that all four fall into the category of "idolization of perceived past experience," the handicap that Revans puts at the top of his list of barriers to learning.

In past experience, learning and curriculum are inextricably bound together, and accountability for learning means guaranteeing its success by means of tests or observations and program evaluation (including cost/benefit analysis). Backward looking often makes it difficult to move on to new perspectives.

While idolization of past experience seems a paradoxical term to apply to new technology and the delivery of content, discussion, and practice elements on-line, a debatable case has been made that e-learning is a warming over of old premises that learners learn most from preplanned menus and robust content, presented well. The only element in learning on the fly that seems to be really new is accessibility of information anytime, anywhere. No one sensibly claims that this ready-to-eat fare will solve all the problems of creating new knowledge.

Belief in the necessity for leader control of learning is certainly of ancient vintage, is well understood, and needs no further explanation. This assumption, together with the other three, hinges on the social perception of education as something done to or on behalf of learners, by those who have taken the responsibility for deciding what learning is needed.

"The impulsion to instant activity" also needs little further explanation. Revans says such impulses are "the managerial equivalent to Gresham's Law: 'Short term issues drive out the long' " (1980, p. 6). The "machines" of the five domains, programmed by whatever visions of the past are extant, are all set to overdrive. Few people would deny that time pressure is a constant presence in their lives.

Revans notes the toll this takes on development of the breadth and depth of understanding needed to solve unprecedented problems. In action learning, participants confront the knowledge that their most valuable insights and willing contributions in their employment outside the set are routinely sacrificed to "instant activity." They become very clear about the need to shift priorities "back home" when they leave the set.

Revans's fourth handicap, "the belittlement of subordinates," has not gone away even though there have been redistributions of power in many organizations. Belittlement is a subtle and persistent fact of life for organizations where "the charismatic influences" of leaders perceived to be successful may override any individual's sense of worth. Clearly these two handicaps (Revans's second and fourth) figure into the perpetuation of the four assumptions about what learning is and what is required for it to happen. There are further effects of charismatic success modeling and other aspects of belittlement cultures that are not treated here because they are more critical to the strategic assessment of contexts in Chapter 3.

HYPOTHESIZING RELATIVE STRENGTHS OF THE FOUR ASSUMPTIONS

We reiterate: persons seeking to introduce action learning in any of the five domains can expect to encounter the four assumptions that seem to have their origins in discipline-based education. If each assumption—curriculum dominance, leader control, learning guarantees, and learning on the fly—was distributed by effect within each of the domains, what would the patterns look like?

Thinking in percentages and drawing upon experiences in

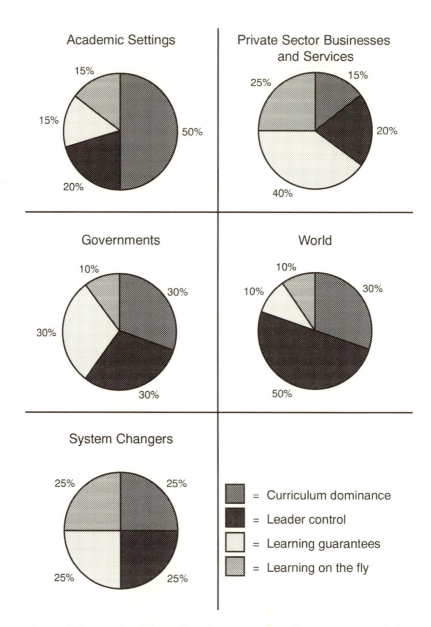

Figure 2.2 Relative Strengths of Assumptions that Negatively Influence Action Learning Adoption.

many different organizational settings, we present in Figure 2.2 an impression of what research might find regarding the relative strengths of the four assumptions that might collectively be acting as barriers to introduction of action learning in each domain. Remember that these pie charts are offered for reflective purposes and not as scientific evidence.

Recognizing that there must be considerable variance in settings even within a single domain (for example, manufacturers and private sector service providers may have profiles that look a bit different), dominance of some assumptions over others may hold clues as to where the greatest sources of resistance to action learning might lie in any particular domain.

Academic Settings

The bias toward curriculum may understandably dominate in the academic settings, although leader control is also likely to be very strong. Learning guarantees and learning on the fly technologies are running neck and neck in the competition to convey more information to more people in less time and with fewer faculty (e.g., growth of e-learning and distance learning). One university delivers 100 percent of its master's degrees in human resource development on-line. Students never meet or interact face to face with their professors.

Private Sector Businesses and Services

In private sector businesses and services, the dominant assumption is that organizations must have learning guarantees. The demand for learning on the fly is erupting, at the same time diminishing leader control over learning. Interest in curriculum has always been primarily a means to the end of guaranteed, instrumental learning and thus the curriculum bias is suppressed by the learning guarantee imperative.

Governments

Government agencies may be fairly even-handed in their biases toward curriculum, leader control, and learning guarantees. A lag in learning on the fly may be attributable to bureaucratic organizational structures that tend to retard change.

World

In international organizations, many competing cultural preferences are involved. Curriculum, leader control, and learning guarantee biases will all be important. Learning on the fly may be longed for, and therefore constitute a bias, but it cannot be said to dominate. It is often still beyond the reach of technology-poor nations that are not yet able to capitalize on the "airport food" style of information delivery. Leader control may wield the heaviest influence, since the didactic tradition is very strong in most nations of the world (including our own).

System Changers

System changers are hardly all alike, but as grouped in a domain there appears to be fairly even support for all four assumptions. If system changers are not individually biased as stated, then their practice across many different kinds of organizations will still tend to even out the biases they encounter and must deal with, if they are to introduce action learning successfully.

In action learning, the deeper one travels into one's own ignorance of the problem nexus, the greater the possibilities of learning *and* problem resolution. This often involves reflecting upon what has already been reflected upon. And so in this chapter we dug deeper into analysis of what we already thought we knew would lie behind resistances we could encounter in different types of organizations. Typically we see ourselves not only in many of the other contexts, but also as system changers and therefore subject to dealing with the four assumptions on many different fronts.

ACTION LEARNING AS REPERTOIRE OF TEACHING/LEARNING COMMUNITIES

Because action learning works, it has growing impact on society and institutions, local to global in scope. It can be made to work better, if a critical mass of adult educators, HRD practitioners, and others concerned with learning at the rate of change become familiar with its natural strengths and dedicate themselves to finding venues for its use. Action learning ought to take its place in the repertoire of teaching/learning communities wherever they exist for some of the following reasons:

1. **It resolves deep-seated real problems or at least sheds new light on directions to take.** Often, the most valued learning is that there are multiple perceptions of any given situation, and that sometimes the "solution" lies in keeping perspectives wide and options open.

2. **It provides clear, strategic "human context" as counterbalance and complement to electronic/hyper-technological explosion in schools, in work, and in society.** Many people react to the technology revolution with mixed feelings, alternately feeling "driven by the machines" and isolated by them, and grateful for the technological support systems that help them do the work. An example of technology imbalance is the work supervision of employees entirely by e-mail—a particularly dehumanizing experience. In the context of action learning, however, people are reinforced in their humanity, learning that they are "good company" even when alone.

3. **It induces personal growth and the integration of learning at a profoundly felt and internalized level hard to come by in the electronic or traditional classroom.** Participants remember critical incidents, specific insights, and "ah-hah" moments vividly, long after the sets have disbanded. Many stay

in close touch for years afterward, continuing to learn with and from each other. This bonding effect is rarely achieved when learners communicate through the veil of technology.

4. **It offers a valuable transitional experience from school to work, and greater confidence in dealing with life's challenges.** Even though most participants in our experience have been adults, many are in school, working, but often in transition and with uncertain futures. Action learning convinces them that they can handle complex situations, fraught with many unknowns.

5. **It changes mental sets and perspectives, challenging false assumptions as well as validating human experience and its meaning for individuals.** A common finding in our critical incident research is that persons who previously felt they were "listeners" and could make no significant contribution are validated by action learning as "people with ideas." They are amazed when they learn that someone else shares their opinion or view of a situation.

6. **It raises the level of internalized learning—learning that sticks throughout life.** Working on genuine problems and engaging in unusually forthright interactions with others produce internalized learning, highly resistant to decay. Growth, the very opposite of decay, occurs instead. Follow-up studies of action learning provide clear evidence that what has been learned, regardless of whether it is about the process or the problem, about valuing others' points of view, or about self, will tend to increase in strength and importance over time. New knowledge continues to be internalized and acted upon. Action learners learn how to learn.

7. **It greatly enhances self-efficacy and perceptions of future success.** It is the rule, not the exception, that action learners become progressively more confident and ready to "take on the world."

8. **It requires making positive assumptions about, and having faith in, participants as adults with extraordinary capacity**

to work and learn simultaneously. Action learning has direct and immediate application, and a single, well-conceived experience of it leaves participants with huge amounts of learning and a taste for more.

SUMMARY

In action learning, periods of P (in this case, the laying out of what action learning is and why it matters) should always suggest counterpoints of reflection upon the learning path just traversed. Reflection is often encouraged by the keeping of learning journals or by making room for quiet thought, but it can also be catalyzed by dialogue, by further reading, by flashes of insight, or by almost anything in the human experience.

This chapter concerned itself with (1) reflections about the assumptions and biases that shape our habits of thought and action regarding learning itself, and (2) reflections about the nature of the environments in which action learning has been or may shortly be introduced.

Reflections may take any form, direction, or frequency that fits the reflector and encourages the deepening of understanding about action learning. Notoriously nonlinear, reflections wind our thinking in and out of tacit knowledge and fresh information in unpredictable ways, raising the likelihood that questions will come to us that may never have been asked by anyone before. Old beliefs are at least temporarily suspended, because the assumptions that fed them are undergoing new tests.

Although designing a "perfect" action learning event may be illusory, practitioners should not be deterred from trials and experimentation with the process regardless of their domain or context. There is much to be gained by experimentation. As long as the cardinal principles are adhered to, then confidence in using the process can be built trial by trial, and benefits for participants and their organizations will become increasingly visible.

In principle, there are no known limitations on the applicability of action learning whatever the recalcitrant problem, the reasons for learning, the culture, or the environment. Wherever there are outcroppings of problems that the people affected don't quite understand and therefore don't quite know how to solve, there is logically a place for action learning.

In practice, however, applications of action learning are conditioned or prevented by various forms of resistance. While barriers to adoption and implementation may often seem more formidable than they actually are, one can hardly assume that action learning will always be welcomed or that, if attempted, it will always be an unqualified success.

Perhaps because action learning is congruent with natural acts and natural processing of new insights in any context, it is often dismissed as some sort of vague, experiential "learning by doing" and therefore not judged appropriate for learning under conditions of stress or urgency. On the contrary, such conditions may make people more receptive than ever to action learning, especially if they have "tried everything else." It is then that action learning can potentially play its most strategic role.

Action learning is purposeful, is not confined to any particular setting, and is responsive to deeply felt personal and organizational needs. As Revans insists,

> The search for those purposes that are enduringly valid demands that the chosen program of learning is not merely a set of maneuvers out there, beyond and alienated from the self... [The search] must offer to each individual student the fulfillment of needs finally discovered at the core of his personality (1972, p. 100).

Revans asserts that action learning demands a commitment to honesty and regard for others. To be honest and unpretentious in the inquiry process requires constant refinement of self-knowledge, accomplished through listening to and entertaining other points of view, giving oneself over to reflecting upon the vitality of all that is said and done, and discovering what is pertinent about the unsaid in any problem situation. No one remains untouched. Already we have seen that such critical reflection and personal "remodeling" have been a hallmark of action learning from the very beginning.

Revans's three interacting systems are central to understanding what he means by action learning. System Alpha is his expression for the opening salvo of inquiry into the problem, its history and manifestations, what keeps it from being solved, and what can be tried to change the situation. System Beta, addressed in fuller detail in Chapter 5, literally describes action learning as science-in-progress. System Gamma, however, insists that it is ultimately the quality of the interplay among and within the specific contexts, the set members, and the individual learner that inhibits or enables action learning. Gamma is the essence of critical reflection — built into action learning by definition, as noted earlier. Reflection is not an additive to make the sets run better or to crank up the problem-solving power.

All three of Revans's systems, together with a firm sense of their mutual necessity and interdependence, are evident in the following declaration [insertions by authors]:

> There is no responsibility either in conjecture or hypothesis, [Alpha] but only in the visible action to verify or refute what is believed [Beta]. And thus the authentic teacher encourages self-discovery by exploiting the stresses of responsible action, evaluation of results, and consequential changes in belief or behavior, the whole sequence of personal involvement in real world problems, value-loaded, complex, and threatening [Alpha, Beta, and Gamma] (Revans, 1972, p. 98).

System Gamma is given next to no attention in contemporary explanations of action learning. This means, of course, that one-third of Revans's premises are negated by omission. This is a critical loss that is avoidable only if action learning programs are planned with Gamma in mind. Personal and collective habits of thought and the effects these have simply cannot be left out of consideration in the learning equation.

CHAPTER 3

Contextual Implications of Action Learning: Lessons Learned

Learning, like eating, is universal. However, how people learn varies from culture to culture. Action learning, developed and practiced primarily in Western countries, needs to be "acculturized," that is, conveyed and transferred across cultural boundaries to assure that the action learning program is, to use a computer term, "user friendly." This does not mean that the essential elements of action learning are dropped or radically altered; rather, they are adjusted to the cultural milieu so as to ensure that the maximum benefits of action learning can be tapped . . . Without this acculturalization and adaptation, the power and benefits of action learning will not be realized.
—Michael J. Marquardt (1999, p. 125)

Context is always important in introducing any form of learning or change to an organization. Specific contexts differ in terms of their readiness to serve as a platform for action learning. However, context seems even more important than customary in the case of action learning. For several reasons, action learning can be viewed as counterintuitive and out of step with traditional educational and training methods. First, it involves empowering workers to a much greater extent than found in most learning initiatives. This can create a conflict with the corporate culture, especially if it is hierarchically oriented and centered on control. Action learning can also find itself in conflict with cultural norms in countries where didactic styles of learning and learner passivity are expected.

Receiving classroom instruction is far removed from unleashing employees to take on real organizational problems of great significance and complexity. Middle-level executives, even some of the more senior ones, can consider the turnover of major problems to employees to solve as an indictment of their own ability to deal with such issues. The more the organizational culture centers on "command and control" mechanisms and power structures to manage the enterprise, the more difficult it can be for action learning to gain entry and to take hold.

FAILED APPLICATIONS OF ACTION LEARNING

Example 1. Insufficient Preparation of the Organizational Culture

One regional organization of a large U.S. corporation decided to inaugurate an action learning initiative. The preparatory work was completed, and management professed to understand the ramifications of employing action learning. A strong commitment was also made to the workforce. Top management announced that they stood behind the initiative, including the empowerment of employees. The workforce took this commitment to heart and, through the action learning process, they proceeded to challenge the way things were being done across the organization. After all, this is what top management said they expected to see happen. As the Pygmalion Effect suggests (Livingston, 1998), what leaders ask for, assuming they have credibility, they can expect to receive. The degree of challenge coming from the workforce became threatening to top management, who quickly backed off from their commitment and quashed the program.

After this kind of event, it can be difficult to reestablish trust with your employees. You need to understand the context before attempting to introduce major change. In the case just described, it is rather obvious that top management did not have the necessary level of buy-in that comes from fully understanding what is involved even in their own context.

Example 2. Management Disinterest and Rigidity of Organizational Culture

The failure of action learning cited above occurred in an organizational context and culture supposedly ready to receive it. In other cases, it can be a situation where neither the culture of the organization nor top management's style of leadership supports the introduction of action learning. Dilworth was brought in by a major corporation to lay the foundation for introduction of work-outs, a form of action learning used successfully by General Electric (GE) and described later in this chapter. A comprehensive study of the corporate environment beforehand, by a major consulting firm, had revealed a number of systemic problems, among them overcentralization of authority, lack of employee empowerment, and blocked lines of communication (organizational arteriosclerosis) because of the highly rigid and hierarchical manner of managing the enterprise. A decision to use action learning stemmed from the belief that the work-outs could effectively combat these reported maladies.

An advance meeting was held with the top leadership of the company to make certain that their expectations were properly aligned with what the consultants felt needed to happen. The chief executive officer (CEO) began the meeting by asking what he could expect in the way of outcomes from the program. Dilworth cited greater decentralization of decision making and greater employee empowerment as two intended outcomes. The CEO responded, "Why would I want to empower the employees?" The CEO also seemed distracted and not that interested in the initiative being addressed. Dilworth, at this point, decided to terminate the consulting work.

A short time later, a senior human resource person in the company called and pleaded for reinstatement of the consultative contract. She was extremely apologetic, said the CEO had been having a bad day when the initial meeting occurred, and that he really did understand and support the effort. A pilot test of the initiative was negotiated. What the pilot served to show was that top management had a mental set and style of leadership that was diametrically opposed to action learning. The organizational culture also resisted an intervention of this type. The program was quickly closed down. While the context in which action learning was to occur seemed appropriate, including the reasons for desiring such an initiative, the culture of the organization and its leadership did not fit well with action learning.

OTHER CONTEXTUAL/CULTURAL RESISTANCES

Many companies, including the one just cited, decide to try the GE-style work-out because of its great success at GE, a corporation long involved with action learning. Jack Welch, the legendary CEO of GE, was once asked by the CEO of another company for advice on introducing the GE-style work-out in his company. Welch reportedly told him, "You had better have a robust culture to begin with!" This advice certainly fits the case and situation just described.

Other resistances to action learning that crop up can relate to assigning people to work on problems with which they are unfamiliar. This can seem illogical, even strange. "Why would I want to take several of my senior executives, well schooled in X, and assign them to work on Y, when they know little or nothing about Y?"

The answer lies in the triggering of fresh questions and in inducing people to question their basic underlying assumptions. There is usually no incentive to do deep introspection in the time-driven environments of U.S. companies. If a problem is involved, it usually has been addressed in some form previously. There is little motivation to search for new understandings.

It is when we find ourselves confronted with an unfamiliar challenge, with all its uncertainties and risks, that we are encouraged to critically examine our own thought processes. This is the foundation on which action learning rests. It can serve as a fulcrum for personal growth. It can also strengthen critical skills, such as those related to problem solving, teamwork, conflict resolution, and leadership.

Another contextual/cultural resistance to action learning can take the form of reluctance to practice adult learning principles, among them, allowing people to function as adults, as opposed to being dependent on instructors for cues and guidance. One of the most resistant contexts can be higher education, where the mode of learning delivery can be a lecture to a multitude of students, with little chance of interaction. It can be a continuation of the pedagogy of K-12 education. Knowledge can be conveyed as a given and not subject to reinterpretation or challenge. To have students interact in subgroups/action learning sets in relation to real problem solving can seem far removed from the norm.

Dilworth and Willis regularly employ students in action learning sets within and outside the classroom. Dilworth was once confronted by a fellow professor who said: "When I walk by your classroom, the students are often in small groups talking to each other. You are usually sitting at the other end of the room looking very relaxed. I even saw them laughing on one occasion. Have you given up teaching?"

The response given was that the focus was on learning, and that formal classroom instruction was only one option, not the only one. The other professor was ensconced in what can be viewed as traditional classroom instruction, a paradigm almost entirely predicated in his mind on P, and essentially the one-way communication of an expert. The act of teaching was the same as learning to him. In the corporate world, training programs can have a similar orientation, one where formal learning and carefully crafted and choreographed curricula hold sway over everything else.

The act of restricting most learning approaches to formal delivery of instruction is usually done with the best of intentions. It is, as Jack Mezirow would say, a "habit of mind." It has become, in some cases, too deeply engrained to be questioned. It can also be comfortable to the instructor. Many are accustomed to formal learning and have no real interest in trying something new. Further, to conduct the learning experience in less formal ways can seem like removing the mantle of expertise and authority over the learner.

Perhaps the most significant contextual barrier to introduction of action learning is a win-lose mentality in relation to power. Supervisors can conclude that their power base will be eroded, and their job security threatened, if employees are set loose to address the resolution of major problems. This resistance can be intense, especially in the ranks of middle managers, a constant target of corporate downsizing in recent years. They have a natural and well-founded basis for being wary. The message that their role can be enhanced through action learning can fall on deaf ears.

In all truth, action learning can lead to streamlining of operations, displacement of people, and realignment of who does what, with more authority migrating to members of the workforce. It is often a move from hierarchical power structures to those that are more heterarchical in nature, with power broadly diffused. This increases the ability of the organization to respond rapidly to change. Action learning can be seen as a change agent for this kind of transformation. One of the reasons GE moved to work-outs was to transform the culture and, as Jack Welch has stated, to "jimmy the locks" of the bureaucratic encumbrances to change (Stewart, 1991, p. 41).

Schein's Cultural Forms of Resistance

As a subtlety in deciphering the readiness of a specific content and culture to receive action learning, you need to bear in mind that the dynamics within the organization are only part of the story. Edgar Schein (1997) addresses this phenomenon in *Three Cultures of Management: The Key to Organizational Learning in the 21st Century.* Schein has identified the operator culture, which is the internal culture of the organization. But there are two other cultures as well, and both come from outside the organization.

The first external influence of organizational culture he calls the executive culture. What influences the chief executive officers and top management comes from the influence of the wide community of business leaders. The second external influencer is what Schein calls the engineering culture, which draws from the worldwide occupational community. A good example of the latter culture can be found in higher education, where what professors do can be driven by the "publish or perish" emphasis and the pursuit of individual goals that promote achievement of tenure. To bring home Schein's point in relation to higher education, you can ask that professors become highly collaborative and begin to operate in teams. In this case, the resistance can be fierce, even if somewhat masked, because downplaying of individual goals can lead to an inability to be hired by other universities In this instance, the vision of the organization can be in sharp conflict with what the employees are willing to buy into and support.

COMMITMENT TO ACTION LEARNING AT GE: LARGE-SCALE CHANGE

The work at GE has been previously cited as an impressive, almost ideal example of the successful contextualizing of action learning processes and principles. Introducing change at GE centered on the introduction of work-outs. This is a very early adaptation of action learning in a U.S. corporation and as such is highly illustrative. The GE effort incorporated broad-based support for and understanding of commitment to organizational change, encouragement of risk taking, championing of specific change efforts, and desire for organizational turnabout. The fact that it was driven from the very top of the organization, in the person of the CEO himself, certainly communicated the urgency of the necessity for change. Reviewing this effort, Marquardt acknowledges that:

> Probably one of the best-known and most successful of all corporate action learning programs is GE's work-out . . . Among the key goals of work-out are:
> - Solving critical system-wide problems.
> - Improving responsiveness to customers.
> - Minimizing vertical and horizontal barriers. (1999, p. 65)

Dilworth's first exposure to work-out occurred when he read a *Washington Post* article entitled, "Seeking a Better Way: With Cutting Edge Tool, GE's Chief Aims to Forge a Boundaryless Firm." The cutting edge tool was the work-out. The article stated: "Less than two years after the first work-out session, they have become a pervasive part of GE's culture—nearly 1,000 work-outs involving 50 or so employees each, have taken place since the process was started" (Potts, October 7, 1990).

Within two months, and moving forward with only the rudimentary details contained in the *Washington Post* article, Dilworth began to use work-outs within the large organization he headed. He found it to be a powerful approach to action learning, although some may contend that it fails to meet all the tests, such as making adequate provision for a reflective component. Such arguments fail to understand the ingredients of a work-out and how they line up with Revans's philosophy. From involvement with work-outs over time, gaining early insights from pioneers of "the work-out technology," including Steve Kerr, Mary Ann Von Glinow, Jeff Kerr, and Clyde Keller, it is patently obvious to Dilworth that the methodology covers key bases of action learning. It involves *real* problems, risk taking, championing of change and transformation of organizational culture.

Why did GE turn to work-outs? One primary reason was Jack Welch's observation that what was covered in programs at their premier corporate university in Crotonville, New York, ended up running into the stone walls of bureaucracy within the company at large. Creativity ended up being stifled rather than promoted. Welch and Jim Baughman, manager of corporate management development at the time, wondered if there was a way " . . . where [employees] could get in front of their leadership and not have retribution. 'Work-out' was settled on as a way of achieving this end" (Potts,1990).

What characterizes a GE work-out and why can it be considered both a prime organizational change/organization development (OD) strategy and powerful expression of action learning principles? Tichy and Sherman indicate that:

> Work-out began in October 1988. The first stage was a series of local gatherings patterned after New England town meetings. In groups of 30 to 100, the hourly and salaried employees of a particular business would spend three days at an off-site conference

center discussing their common problems. No coats. No ties. The setting and behavior were so different from business as usual that work-out consultant, Steve Kerr, called these meetings "unnatural acts in unnatural places." (1993, p. 201)

The reference to unnatural acts in unnatural places lines up well with Revans's emphasis on unfamiliar problems in unfamiliar settings (contexts). Work-outs within GE generated some immediate resistances:

Some mistakenly thought the name was meant to justify further downsizing. They feared that work-out meant "taking out" people. To such carping Welch and Baughman said, "Indulge us." (Slater, 1993, p. 214)

Another sign that work-out is a form of action learning is that a work-out starts with the selection of real problems that need addressing. During the early days of the work-out at GE, the focus was on removal of needless bureaucracy. Later, it could involve process mapping. Participants for a work-out could be either from one corporate entity, or preferably from different cross-functional entities in order to break down boundaries to communication (GE's "boundaryless company").

Because the GE version provides many insights into the contextualizing of action learning, it may be helpful to provide a generalized overview of the three-day work-out. Similar processes could work successfully in many other kinds of organizations, if the will to change the culture and work of the organization is strong. The following example, drawn from Dilworth's firsthand experience and involvement, included 32 participants. The events are described day by day, to demonstrate how the flow of activity can be organized.

Day 1
- Participants assemble early in the morning.
- The senior leader involved briefly addresses the group, expresses full support for the process, and then leaves.
- Facilitators provide some opening exercises to motivate creativity and engagement.
- The work-out process is explained.

Contextual Implications of Action Learning   65

- Participants are broken into ad hoc groups of six to eight people and asked to determine what they view as some principal improvements needed in the organization. Participants then vote on issues raised across groups in arriving at those that the overall group feels need highest priority. These charts are displayed on the main conference room walls throughout the work-out.
- The overall group is broken down into teams of eight people, in this case four teams (action learning sets in Revans's parlance). Each set meets in a separate room with a facilitator. The facilitator jump-starts the process and then, to the extent possible, fades back and assumes more of an observer role.
- Each group is fully empowered to arrive at two to four proposals related to the issue/problem it is to address. Each of the groups can be given a different area (e.g., customer service, improvement of order processing).
- Each proposal developed is entered on *one* overhead slide using a grease pencil. Entries include: Issue, Symptoms, Recommendations, Benefits, Action Plan, Potential Obstacles, and Champions (not confined to the work-out team).
- To help team members determine specific proposals to be pursued, the value matrix displayed in Figure 3.1 is commonly used.
- Team culls down its proposals to just a few. The "High Payoff, Easy to Implement" quadrant of the value matrix is a prime hunting ground. Within GE, it has been called low-hanging fruit.
- Team begins to refine each proposal into a form that can be presented for decision in three to four minutes.

Day 2
- Team rehearsals continue.
- In the afternoon, each team presents its proposals (a designated spokesperson) to the entire group (all four teams) and the facilitators. One of the facilitators acts out the kind of questions that the top leader may ask in receiving the presentation. All proposals must be accepted by the *full group* to be presented. Therefore, the entire group stands behind each and every proposal to be presented.

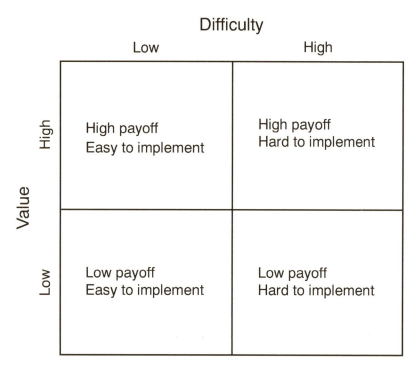

Figure 3.1 Value Matrix for Evaluating Possible Recommendations (A similar matrix has been used during the GE work-out process.)

Day 3
- The leader arrives for the presentation of proposals and decision making. The leader may be escorted past the charts displaying principal issues arrived at on the first day in the early practice session (i.e., areas in which the organization needs to improve.)
- One of the facilitators maintains tight time discipline. It is commonplace for as many as 20 proposals to be presented for decision within two hours.
- As each proposal is presented, the leader must reach a decision then and there. There are only three choices: approve, reject, or defer (usually for no longer than 30 days). Rejection or deferral must be explained. It cannot be a case of rejection without comment. The leader is asked to write the decision and sign the overall slide with grease pencil, on the spot.

The Power of Championed Decisions

To understand the power of the moment, when the decision making occurs, you really need to experience it. It can be akin to the Super Bowl for the participants, some of whom may not have experienced such empowerment before. The atmosphere is charged, electric. It is the ultimate test of the leader. Credibility is on the line. Should the leader show hesitancy or lack of knowledge, his or her credibility can sink.

Dilworth was at a work-out presentation (not GE-related) in Tallahassee, Florida. When asked to approve a proposal to implement a new procedure by December, the leader said, "Approved, but not until next June." There was immediate hissing and foot stomping to demonstrate that the timetable for implementation was unacceptable. Some chanted "December, December!" Unnerved, the leader said, "Okay." The hissing turned to cheering. You must be a strong and capable leader to weather such a face-off with employees. It represents a leadership development experience for the leader. While the circumstance just described is probably an extreme case, it is not an anomaly in terms of the intense views held by the employees. It is said at GE that if the boss is standing behind the leader receiving the proposals and making decisions, it is extremely bad form to turn around to gauge the top leader's facial expressions regarding support for the proposal. The leader is expected to be capable of making the decisions without reference to others.

When such a process fails, as it did in the Tallahassee example, it has often been undermined by a failure of leadership. The Tallahassee attempt occurred in state government. The employees were ready for empowerment. On the other hand, it frightened the leaders. They stopped with the one work-out experience, even though there were clear signs that it had been high impact and had led to some significant and very positive changes.

In contrast, what is visible in the GE experience with work-out is:

1. Strong commitment from the top was present (the CEO having been instrumental in design of the strategy).

2. Risk taking occurred per the design of the work-out approach. The employees stood together as a group, somewhat reducing the risk to individuals in expressing contrarian views.

3. Championing was provided for. The groups could designate individuals outside the group, having consulted with them by telephone while deliberating on various proposals. Revans points out in addressing the issue of implementation that you need three types of people (or champions) involved—those who care, those who can, and those who know.

4. Organizational turnabouts can occur. GE has not only transformed its culture but also planted the seeds of on-going cultural renewal.

5. While reflection is not treated as a distinct ingredient of the work-out methodology, it is easy to see that it does, in fact, occur. Any witness to the process observes that there is much soul searching, and it extends to the implementation phase following a work-out.

Outcomes of Work-out Types of Action Learning

How many employee recommendations get approved during work-outs at GE? It usually exceeds 85 percent. The proposals are usually not wild-eyed. They have had to pass muster across the entire work-out assembly, not just the team level. On balance, the proposals tend to be a stretch beyond what proposals usually contain. Fresh questions have been asked, a cross-section of perspectives brought together, and the participants extremely motivated.

Certainly there are employee and management development implications. In 1992, GE inaugurated the change acceleration program (CAP) as "a systematic attempt to use work-out to breed a new type of GE manager" (Tichy & Sherman, 1993, p. 209). Like other GE initiatives with an action learning core, CAP found its way into other organizations eager to emulate the GE success. One of these organizations was the Federal Deposit Insurance Corporation (FDIC). Writing on "Accelerated Decision-Making via Action Learning at the FDIC," an initiative that is modeled after GE's CAP, Lanahan and Maldonado indicate that action learning is used within the FDIC context in two ways:

1. As a principal component of core training for executives and managers through the Management Excellence Program.
2. as an organizational problem-solving method, referred to as accelerated decision making, which is facilitated by the FDIC's training and consulting organization (1998, p. 75).

In the case of the program at FDIC, reflection is built into the process. Following the presentation to decision-makers (as addressed earlier in explaining the work-out approach), one hour is set aside to "debrief the process" (p. 79). The facilitator leads the group in reflecting on what worked well, what could have been done better, what to recommend for the future, and how to overcome obstacles during implementation. What tends to be missing here, though, are questions related to what individual learning occurred. What did participants leave with that was not part of their makeup when they entered? Did they have cause to fundamentally change any of their beliefs/underlying assumptions as a result of the process?

REVIEWING BEST PRACTICES IN OTHER ORGANIZATIONS

The examples from GE can be considered best practices, but not all best practices are found in the United States. One of the most impressive models is found in Scandinavia at the Management Institute of Lund (MIL) in Sweden. "MIL works both internally in Sweden and with 30 international corporations from the Nordic countries to run a Scandinavian Management Program" (Marsick & Cederholm, 1988).

Founded in 1977, the MIL bases its programs on "action-reflection-learning," a modality also used by the Leadership in International Management (LIM), MIL's sister organization in the United States. It has, from the outset, been directed at the leadership dimension in turbulent times. " . . . It was based on four concepts of leadership (i.e., thriving on changes, living with paradoxes, trust as overruling (but not excluding control) and learning (i.e., action-reflection-learning and real-time strategic projects)" (Introducing the MIL International Newsletter, 1996, p. 4).

Many companies have been involved with the MIL since its formation. From 1979 to 1988, for example, the consortium of businesses working with the MIL had grown from 13 companies to 15 (Marsick & Cederholm, 1988). Companies can submit project proposals to the MIL around which project teams can be formed, composed of high potential executives for participating companies.

> An overwhelming percentage of the participating corporations have also reported usable outcomes from the work done by project groups. As a result, many corporations lobby hard to have their problems selected as team projects. (Marsick & Cederholm, 1988)

Unlike the GE work-out and related CAP programs, a MIL program can characteristically extend over a series of months, with several multiday sessions together.

The MIL example dramatizes the fact that action learning is occurring in the corporate world on a large scale, and has been for some time, because of proven results. The linkage of the action-reflection-learning orientation to the action learning principles espoused by Revans can be seen in four ingredients related to the way action-reflection-learning is designed to stimulate the learners:

1. Gain new experiences by solving real problems.

2. Reflect on experiences—their own and those of others.

3. Develop their own theories for interpretation and action.

4. Mature personally (Rohlin, 1996).

Contextual Implications of Action Learning 71

From an assessment of context perspective, the MIL example shows that you can draw people together from a wide-ranging group of cultures, extending even beyond the bounds of Scandinavia in this case. On the other hand, those participating in the MIL consortium tend to come from an analogous context—private business.

WHAT IS NEW ABOUT ACTION LEARNING AND HOW IT OVERLAPS OTHER APPROACHES

As indicated in Chapter 1, where 24 characteristics of action learning are listed, many of these characteristics can be associated with other modalities as well. Confidentiality and mutual trust, for example, are necessary for collaborative inquiry, the problem-solving model, and organization development, not just action learning. Using a practical approach is certainly not unique to action learning, nor is having learners work on a joint problem.

What can stand out as different about action learning is the challenge of working with unfamiliar problems in unfamiliar settings, but this is not necessarily a staple of action learning, even though it is emphasized by Revans and by us, among others. The majority of action learning programs today tend to be based off-site, away from the work, while engaged in familiar problem solving (that is, a problem frequently drawn from the organization they are with) and the setting they address is still their own familiar one. That can, of course, lead to a meaningful learning experience. GE, on the other hand, has obviously practiced action learning in a way that can lead to address of problems unfamiliar to the learner.

Real problem solving is not unique to action learning, even though the problems addressed can be by design at the outer limits in terms of complexity.

As already suggested, the answer in terms of what distinguishes action learning lies in the mosaic of characteristics associated with it. It has more of these characteristics concurrently operative than probably any other approach to learning. The mosaic is, in turn, surrounded by a strong sense of ethics and respect for human dignity, including a belief that individuals and teams can learn to make a difference. Empowerment becomes real and genuine, practiced not as a form of subtle manipulation, but rather as a way to unleash human creativity. If there is an especially telling word one can associate with action learning, it would seem to be *authenticity*. Great force can flow from that aspect alone, because the climate of organizations can be viewed as harsh and inauthentic. Argyris, Putnam, and Smith point this out in describing the Model I (or MI) that pervades organizations (1985). They draw the distinction between "espoused theory" and "theory-in-use." The four governing variables of the Model I, a model originally conceived by Argyris and Schön in 1974, are:

1. achieve the purpose as the actor defines it;

2. win, do not lose;

3. suppress negative feelings;

4. emphasize rationality (Argyris, Putnam, & Smith, 1985, p. 89).

What typifies Model I is low freedom of choice and defensiveness. You say one thing (espoused theory) and practice something else (theory-in-use). A climate of undiscussability is created. Since many organizations operate this way, according to Argyris, Putnam, and Smith, it represents a barrier to the introduction of action learning. Emphasis on discussability and openness ends up going head to head with cultures that operate on the basis of closed communications.

What all this suggests, once again, is that:

1. You need to understand both the specific context and the specific culture.

2. You will almost always need to prepare the culture before attempting to employ action learning, unless you are willing to accept an MI, superficial, way of operating, where any form of major advance or new thinking is unlikely.

Contextual Implications of Action Learning 73

Gaining Administrative Interest and Support Versus "Going it Alone"

If you consider action learning to be an expression of organization development, and it can be considered as such, then some classic lessons transfer. Action learning is, by its very nature, an organizational change strategy. You can focus your efforts on the broad context (e.g., entire company in the case of GE) or aim an action learning intervention at one specific area within a culture. The ideal approach is to go for a broad intervention with top management support. When you deal with only a relatively small sector of the overall organization, the intervention can get snuffed out quickly by external pressures (and perhaps those internal as well). What doesn't fit the status quo of the overall organization will usually be singled out for rejection. There is a saying in Japanese management that "the nail that sticks out gets hammered."

If you are going for a small area of the culture as a pilot, and there is wisdom in doing so, it is wise to have the overall leadership structure aware and supportive, not just the leadership structure in the area that is directly affected.

Willis is convinced that action learning groups can be productively used in support of a single executive or manager, as a means of moving these leaders toward more open management styles, more collaborative decision making, and greater confidence in their own ability to change the terms of their engagement with real problems. In these instances, with which Willis has several years' experience, the leader is personally a part of the ongoing action learning set that is otherwise composed of graduate students. When the client leaders are at very high levels in the organization, with wide spans of control, they can and do have an impact on the whole organization -including more open communication with their CEO.

There need to be preparatory steps taken to gain support before entering an organization. Action learning can be viewed as "flavor of the month" in some companies. "It has worked at GE and elsewhere. Let's give it a spin!" This can be followed by a rapid-fire intervention, perhaps by those unschooled in action learning (and organizational development, for that matter). The outcome becomes rather predictable. The action learning program may fold almost as quickly as it is set up. A case in point is the example described earlier in the book, where the company decided to use action learning, only to become frightened when employees took empowerment seriously.

In terms of going it alone, that simply doesn't work. Anyone planning to create an action learning program in an organization is going to need advocates, people who understand the risks, advantages, and nuances. That can entail having someone who really understands action learning serve as an advisor, confidant and co-program developer.

What is discussed here is really the initiation phase of action learning, one of three phases (see Chapter 5). If the process is not initiated properly, the likelihood of success becomes doubtful.

Recruiting Participants Versus Making Participation Mandatory

The reflexive, knee-jerk, reaction, when asked whether action learning should be made mandatory or voluntary, is usually an emphatic "voluntary!" The answer is really both, but often beginning with a mandatory program. Because action learning is different, there is a need to get people "into the swimming pool," to test the water. If an organization believes that action learning can bring the kind of advantages often realized, including the development of highly effective leadership cadres and fostering of high-order problem-solving skills, then it should not be hesitant to bring action learning on-stream and require participation.

What GE has learned over time—and it was quite clear that employees were required to participate—is that once you get over the introductory hurdle, employees can take to action learning naturally. It becomes an accepted way of working through tough issues. Further, suborganizations begin to adapt the methodology to their immediate needs—and that is a big plus. Action learning is not an immutable, ironclad template that must follow one pattern to be successful. One of its prime strengths is its ready adaptability.

Moving to Action: Envisioning How to Design a Program So That Action Learning Works

There are several steps you need to go through in designing a program. As indicated repeatedly in this chapter, you must consider the specific context first. The way you introduce action learning in a corporation is not the way you go about introducing it in a community college or state bureaucracy. While organizations can vary in any domain, some being high performing, with others slow to move forward, context plays an important part in the design and implementation of an action learning program.

Once the context is considered, it is important to scope the organization's culture to be entered. This cannot be cursory or dependent upon third-party reports. You need to physically enter the environment and both observe how it operates and talk with people. Top management should head the list in terms of early discussions. If there is no real impetus to act, or they are uncomfortable with action learning when it is explained to them, chances are it will not work. Top management must do more than say they support introduction of action learning. You need to ensure that they really understand it. There is a wonderful story about Peter F. Drucker and his consultancy with a large company. The CEO had recruited Drucker and indicated to him that the project to be pursued (not action learning related) carried with it the very highest priority within the company. At the first meeting of the corporate board to discuss the project, the CEO introduced Drucker and then moved to leave the conference room. When the CEO found Drucker right behind him, he said: "Where are you going"? Drucker said, "If this is all the interest you have in the project, I'm leaving too." Without top leadership support and understanding, the project is doomed.

The selection of the project is also important. It must relate to a real unsolved problem. The client(s) must also be identified. There have been cases of an action learning project being brought to fruition, only to find that no one felt accountable for implementing the results.

One of the stickiest issues relates to the relationship between the action learning set that determines appropriate remedies and the people who end up implementing the remedies. If the action learning set was dealing with an unfamiliar problem, it is reasonable to assume that those who will implement the fixes must come from elsewhere. Why should they buy in to the recommendations being made when they had no part in developing them? Technically, the fixes can involve problems that the experts were ineffective in troubleshooting, and now those same experts can end up being asked to apply someone else's fixes to the problems. That can end up with crossed lines of communication, resistance to change and other significant obstacles to implementation.

In the GE work-out design, provision is made for inclusion of champions early in the process, and they can come from the ranks of those who know (expertise). There is also a case for seeding the set from the beginning with some people who are in the know. However, that can dampen the asking of fresh questions and even work against problem resolution. You can have P in the room that muddles rather than clarifies thinking. The thinking-out-of-the-box properties can end up being diluted.

In the Belgian action learning experiments by Revans, there were linkages created that promoted a smooth transition and clear interface between the identification of the problem and solution and the implementation phase.

Willis notes that, in the case of client managers and executives who are actually part of the action learning set (otherwise composed of complete outsiders), the leaders never lose sight of the fact that they own the problem and will have to attend to implementation. This model of intervention appears to be very close to the Belgian example often cited by Revans. The Belgian example will be discussed at greater length in Chapter 4.

SUMMARY

Everything begins with consideration of assumptions, context, and culture and proceeds from there. You must have top management support and understanding of action learning itself if the program is to be successful.

There are an initiation phase, action learning phase, and implementation phase. Much of what is discussed in this chapter relates to the initiation phase, in that it starts the process, including the scoping of context and organizational culture. In Chapter 5, we will systematically examine each of the three phases/arenas and demonstrate how they interrelate.

CHAPTER 4

The Action Learning Plan

The structure and operational characteristics of a model are determined to a high degree by the purpose it is to serve. The client exercises a legitimate function in determining the characteristics of a model that is being developed for his use. Different models may be equally effective, but not equally practicable when evaluated in terms of the client's aims and resources.
—Stogdill (1970, p. 6)

Three phases drive the overall action learning process: initiation, action learning, and implementation. The initiation phase lays the groundwork, including the assessment of the specific context and culture. This was covered at some length in Chapter 3. We turn our attention now to models of action learning that are commonly used.

SELECTING THE ACTION LEARNING MODEL

The action learning phase begins with selection of the model to use. Two basic action learning models are available. One is the joint project model. Marquardt (1999, p. 42) refers to it as the Single-Project Program. The second we call Everyone Bring One (EBO), which is referred to as the Open-Group Program by Marquardt (p. 43). In the joint project model, as the name infers, all members of the action learning set will be concentrating on one project. In the Everyone Bring One model, each set member brings to the set a problem that is usually taken from that person's work environment.

The model chosen ends up having a significant impact on

group dynamics. In the joint project model, the problem presented to the group is shared in common. It can only be dealt with through collective group synergy. The shared problem binds the group together and generates cohesion. The set can only arrive at a comprehensive understanding of the problem and how to deal with it by sharing knowledge. The joint problem serves as a catalyst in integrating the group.

The dynamics are usually somewhat different in the Everyone Bring One set. First of all, the problems brought to the table by individual set members can be quite uneven in complexity. Politics and "mother nature" (for example, the tendency to avoid unnecessary risks) can enter the process. There is really no incentive to seek highly complex problems to work on. The normal predilection is to seek out something that is both manageable and politically correct. There is no reward in setting yourself up for failure by self-selecting a project of extreme challenge and difficulty. For the reasons cited, the bar can be set relatively low when it comes to individual set members seeking out a meaningful project.

Another difference between the two models relates to the nature of the dialogue. In the sets operating on the joint model, the dialogue tends to distribute itself naturally, depending on issues being addressed and who is prepared to provide ideas. In sets operating on an EBO basis, time available needs to be carved up so that everyone receives "air time" and an opportunity to receive feedback and recommendations from other set members. It can be like a form of catharsis, with each EBO set member using the set as a listening group for personal viewpoints. Figure 4.1 summarizes the characteristics of the two models. Figure 4.2 indicates differences in the two models from the standpoint of challenge and evenness of load.

While there are obvious differences between the two models, both can be effective. Either model tends to be much more potent than what occurs in a traditional classroom because of its link with a real-world problem.

There is, in effect, a third model which superficially can seem to be an offshoot of the EBO model, but the subtleties of it make it quite different. It has its origins in Revans's Belgian project, involving a consortium of universities and large indus-

Advantages and Disadvantages of the Joint Project Model and the Everyone Bring One Model

Model	Advantage	Disadvantage
Joint Project	Is an equal challenge to all set members. Can select unfamiliar problem. Tends to build high commitment level (e.g., not letting colleagues down). Usually leads to joint presentation to client in a team mode, usually with a strong team feeling (all for one, one for all). Having to deal with the unfamiliar can promote creativity.	Can be more difficult to engineer than EBO (e.g., negotiating project and lining up a client). Causes individuals to work on projects that may be of limited interest.
Everyone Bring One (EBO)	Relatively easy to administer since learners line up the problems. Allows the learner to select something of special interest. Can give exposure to multiple issues. Can discover similarities across problems.	Projects can differ widely in level of difficulty. Deals with apples and oranges rather than one challenging problem that all can focus on (tends to diffuse energy). In a sense, everyone is alone. No one is bound up in having to adopt the views of others. Tends to engender less bonding between team members than joint project.

Figure 4.1 Comparison of the Joint Project Model and the Everyone Bring One Model.

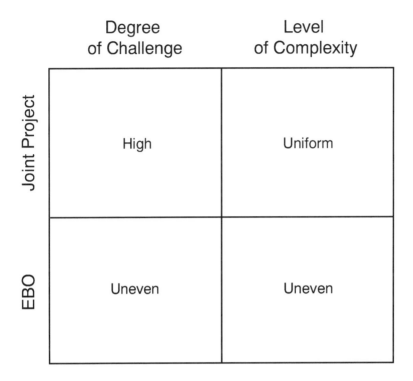

Figure 4.2 Influence of Model Selection on Depth of the Learning Experience

tries in Belgium in the 1960s. To our knowledge, this model has not been used beyond the Belgian project, yet it contains some intriguing properties and was highly successful in Belgium. It is more complex to bring together than the other two models.

The Belgian project involved setting up action learning sets of five senior executives from different industries/business sectors. Each set member was assigned to work on a major problem far removed from that person's normal expertise, conforming to Revans's interest in causing people to be placed in unfamiliar territory. Since set members had not worked together before, that was also an unfamiliar dimension. Like EBO, every set member had a different problem, but it was not from that member's own workplace, nor was it one that set member had picked.

Projects were determined carefully. They had to be of the

insoluble variety. A client organization was identified and a commitment obtained to follow through on implementation of useful findings. Top management of the company also had to commit support and agree to provide any needed corporate resources to the client organization in implementing the results.

One of the members of an initial set was a banker. He was asked to work on a problem involving the largest steel company in Belgium. The problem related to alloy steel, something the banker knew nothing about. The steel company had state-of-the-art manufacturing methods for alloy steel, but it was failing to get the steel out the door in profitable quantities. The marketing effort simply fizzled, and the Japanese were making major inroads in terms of market share. The banker held a series of meetings with steel company employees over a series of months, including top management. He observed, absorbed, and processed what was occurring. In the end, he isolated the problem, one that had escaped notice in earlier attempts at resolution. He found that for well over one hundred years, corporate incentives had been based on tonnage shipped, from the entry-level workers to those in the corporate boardroom. Alloy steel was light. It did not have the weight of pig iron and other forms of steel. Therefore, there was no impetus to move alloy steel. The emphasis was rather on moving the heaviest steel products. Everyone had overlooked the connection between the compensation system, which was supported by the labor unions, and types of steel being shipped.

In the case just cited, and it was a part of the model, a set internal to the client organization, drawing on the findings of the banker, was established to implement the findings. This included revamping the compensation system. Attention was given to including in the set internal to the client those who care, those who know, and those who can (power), as per Revans's philosophy.

During the period that the banker was working on the steel company problem, he was comparing notes with his other set members (external to the steel company), each confronted with an issue of comparable difficulty and outside of the area of expertise. What is significant about this third model is that it provides for interlinkage between the problem scoper/solver and the action learning set that is created to deal with the solution implementation. The use of one set (i.e., a member of it) to troubleshoot the problem and another set to implement the results requires careful advance work. Coming up with five problems of great complexity at the outset and coordinating the action learning effort with the five client groups also constitute complex preparatory work. When you examine the comparative group dynamics of the three models just outlined in terms of set cohesion and team learning, the pattern shown in Figure 4.3 emerges.

A Hybrid Fourth Model Is a Possibility

The hybrid model Willis uses with her graduate students and client organizations seems distinctive enough to constitute yet a fourth model. Each student set works on a single project with a single organization (joint project). That constitutes their primary action learning set. The set meets after work. In this set, the client manager is their only organizational contact, to whom they will formally report. Set members also have the advantage of being able to compare notes among themselves without the client present. Like the problem scopers in the Belgian project, they will not be a hands-on part of a client implementation, nor will they hand the client a full-blown problem solution. But they work directly with the problem owner who is connected to those "who know, who care, and who can" in the client organization, much as the Belgian problem scopers did. This model provides an intimate inside look at organizational assumptions, cultures, contexts, and interconnected issues that students would find hard to come by through any other means. One of the striking aspects of this model is that, although the home set never takes on the responsibility for the problem which they have no organizational jurisdiction to implement, they work at the problem with as much commitment as if they were full-time employees. The key seems to be that the cohesion that builds between the students and the client in their set is built

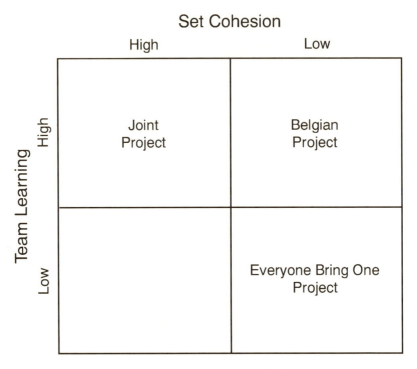

Figure 4.3 Group Dynamics Compared by Project Model

entirely on trust, unaffected by complicating organizational relationships that they are not asked to assume. The action that the client takes usually breaks new ground and is directly applied to the problem the client owns. The action the students take is to inquire, support, challenge, and take intellectual and interpersonal risks that for them are also very high profile and also potentially groundbreaking.

CREATING ACTION LEARNING SETS

This brings us to the issue of set composition. In some cases, little attention is given to who will be in a set. It can be as simple as who happens to be available, or who wants to be in a set with whom. This can lead to constituting action learning sets as cliques. We believe that careful attention to set composition is critical. What is being created is a learning community. To the extent you strive to build a mix of participants of different expertise, gender, ethnicity, and learning style, the learning experience can be strengthened. It can elevate the probability that a problem will get solved. It can also make sense within an organization to include people from different functional areas. Such cross-functionality can help build networks, broaden understanding of business processes (which do not respect corporate boundaries), and help integrate the enterprise. GE goes beyond what most organizations consider in building the diversity of set composition. GE has been known to include customers, suppliers, and even competitors in set composition in order to spark thinking and get people "outside the box."

A company Revans himself had worked with earlier (GEC in the United Kingdom) had led the way in this regard, including set members from outside of the company. At one point the GEC sets involved British postal workers, since the interface problem between the two organizations was related to specifications and orders. In their report on the GEC project, Casey and Pearce spoke of the jolting but fruitful effects of such personnel "swapping" (1977, pp. 79–90).

Determination of set composition is a strategic decision that focuses on maximizing the learning experience and producing a high yield to the organization over time, not just today or tomorrow. It is an effort to increase the capacity of the organization by building employees' self-confidence, as well as broadening and deepening skill sets. It can be an ideal leadership development tool. As at GE, it can be used with the intent to transform the corporate culture and build networks across corporate boundaries, hierarchical as well as cross-functional. Learning goals start the process (e.g., focus on leadership development). Then you turn to steps that constitute the initiation phase, including selection of a problem (in the case of a joint project) and examination of the specific context and culture.

How do you go about determining set composition? As already mentioned, you begin with some strategic learning goals in mind, such as increasing the level of collaborative effort between organizations A and B because they share in the management of some key processes. One way to build such collaboration is to bring together in a set people from both A and B, and then have them work on a very difficult problem impacting their organizations, and possibly others, that set members selected may know little about.

You want to strive for diversity within sets. We will describe an actual process of set determination used in 1996, in England, in establishing five action learning sets of six to seven participants. The population drawn from was primarily from the United States, but also included Canadians and Australians. Some of the learning coaches were British. The participants had almost no familiarity with the specific problems selected for examination by the National Health Service. In this instance, the 31 total participants were a given. They had enrolled in the special program involved. Only two of the participants had deep health service background.

For openers, we wanted the Canadians and Australians equally distributed over the five sets. We wanted gender and ethnicity distributed as well. In addition, we wanted to distribute participants so that the greatest diversity of background was realized in sets. Finally, we wanted to distribute learning styles in a way that created some balance. We used the Honey-Mumford Learning Style Questionnaire (LSQ), which addresses four learning styles: activist, reflector, theorist, and pragmatist. We wanted to avoid a situation where a set would be overwhelmingly skewed toward any one dimension. The LSQ includes whether the individual is very strong, strong, moderate, low, or very low in relation to each dimension. Some individuals turn out to be strong in three or four of the categories. Learning style can be compared with reception of various channels on a TV when it comes to clarity of the picture. A strong inclination to activism can make that channel very clear. On the other hand, a person with a low activist score may see the same screen as "snowy." Such contrasts can influence the quality of communication that occurs in a group. Dilworth has used the LSQ as one signpost for set composition since 1993.

Set composition determinations, when you have so many variables to account for, can be akin to working with a Rubik's Cube. About the time one face of the cube is in color alignment, another falls out of alignment. In this case, you could have the nationalities properly distributed only to find that gender balance in individual sets was uneven. You gradually work with the mix until it seems to be as diverse and balanced as you are likely to achieve. You can also use other collateral data to determine set composition.

Here are two specific examples from the 1996 set composition determinations in England. They reflect not only the diversity measures already mentioned, but also conscious attention paid to potential group dynamics and how given individuals could be placed in the best environment for learning.

Example 1. One set had an individual who had demonstrated in earlier group activities a propensity for trying to gain dominance over others in a group. We purposely placed in that group someone whom we knew would counter such a problem if it arose. It did not arise, possibly because the person inclined to dominate sensed there was a counterforce in the set.

Example 2. One participant was extraordinarily introverted and rarely expressed herself. She had scored zero on the LSQ in the activist area, something that is quite rare. She was a CPA. We purposely placed her in a group that would be dealing with high-level issues regarding financial planning for the National Health Service. This provided a problem focus where she could bring her special skills to bear, even though the problem was outside the bounds of what she was accustomed to addressing. She ended up getting an opportunity to contribute, seized it, received accolades from other set members as well as the client, and ended up volunteering to present a portion of the findings to top management. She said later that volunteering to present was like an "out of body" experience. It just was not what she expected herself to do. She also confided that having her contribution so favorably recognized had a major impact on her. Very little praise had been directed her way in her life, and, therefore, she had adopted a style of rarely speaking.

ESTABLISHING TIME FRAMES

The amount of time to be set aside for action learning is an important consideration. The complexity and scope of the project selected also figure in. As outlined in Chapter 3, the GE work-outs normally extend to only three days, and yet can be considered action learning. Some will contend that three days is insufficient to constitute true action learning. They will argue that it requires six to nine months, yet, in some instances, the actual face-to-face contact time between set members can be less over six months than it is in a three-day GE style work-out. It is not uncommon in some approaches, lasting several months, for a set to meet for two hours every two weeks.

The intensity of the effort obviously needs to be taken into account. We run action learning programs that last roughly four months, with sets meeting officially for three hours once a week. However, the sets will frequently have up to two additional sessions a week of equivalent length in doing their work. It is an intense experience. It is clear that merely addressing the overall time envelope involved is an imperfect index. We shy away from setting guidelines for what is an appropriate time interval. Marvin Weisbord, co-developer of the Future Search Conference methodology with Sandra Janoff, which is close in form and dynamics to action learning, runs 16 1/2-hour Future Search Conferences over three days, yet it is extremely powerful and can impact an organizational culture.

There is a need to consider the magnitude of a joint project in relation to available time of the set to work on it. As a rule of thumb, the set needs to find itself having to stretch to complete the project in the time allotted. You want the set to be challenged, and if the problem is in fact a critical one needing earliest resolution, there should be a sense of time urgency present. Consideration needs to be given to the time required for data gathering and analysis in arriving at deadlines. The Everyone Bring One model tends to complicate the time equation because there isn't just one horse in the race. There are multiple projects underway, which will unavoidably require somewhat different time spans to address properly. It can technically be a case of calibrating expected time for project completion on the basis of the problem resolution expected to take the longest. Here you see another pitfall of the EBO model.

Considering the hybrid model utilized by Willis, it may also be a pitfall to assume that the data collection will be done by the set itself or that the problem will be completely "peeled and solved" in the time allotted. Some action learning efforts may be erroneously considered "failures" if "product" is not delivered. This perspective downplays the enormous value of the learning about self and others in action learning, whether or not the contentious problem is "solved." The very best outcome in some instances may be a recognition that a problem may be unavoidable but can be mitigated by various means.

ENGAGEMENT OF SETS AND CLIENTS

Engagement tends to occur more quickly within sets when they find themselves at the deep end of the pool having to deal with a joint project that is extremely challenging. Engagement and, for that matter, set cohesion, when the EBO model is used, tends to be less taut. The urgency of project completion usually does not enjoy the same level of pressure. It can also be difficult for one set member to judge the nature of someone else's self-identified project. There is not a unity of purpose or a sense that close cooperation is necessary for success.

Engagement of the client is an equally important issue and it can be a delicate one, especially when determining a joint project. It will usually be difficult to engage the client deeply in the philosophy of action learning. The attractiveness of action learning to the client turns first of all on the promise that a perplexing problem of importance will have new light shed upon it, and may be brought to resolution. The client usually plans out of a task-specific orientation. There are other issues as well. Will the client actually be able to be responsive to the set when it needs information in pursuing its analysis? We have experienced situations where the client ended up caught up in other tasks of immediate urgency and could not devote attention to action learning set requests for data. This does not necessarily suggest that the client's level of engagement or commitment has faltered, or that the client was less than honest when parameters of the project were set. The client is probably being battered by the winds of reality. In 2001, Dilworth experienced a situation where sales for the client organization suddenly plummeted because of an economic downturn, causing the organization to close its doors. This was certainly disruptive, but when you deal with the real world, you expect to be impacted by real world events. In the case just cited, all but one member of the set scored the experience as a tremendous learning opportunity. One said: "It doesn't get more real than this! I got a picture of what it's really like in a high tech company." Pursuit of problem resolution may have "gone bust" and had to be truncated, but the learning involved was probably heightened, even with the high level of frustration the set experienced.

Willis believes that the hybrid model that incorporates the client manager in the set serves to keep both the data collection and the problem resolution in the client's own ball court and gives that client the power, exponentially raised through set learning, to produce phenomenal accomplishments. Leading in complex organizations can be a lonely business, yet here are six intelligent individuals willing to dedicate themselves to you, your information needs, testing of your assumptions, and progressive inquiry about your problem for hours every week! Client executives and managers report that it is an experience like no other, affirming and encouraging the best in them.

You cannot get around some of the potential problems in dealing with a client, such as external factors relating to a souring economy, but you can arrive at basic understandings. It is extremely important to strike a memorandum of understanding (MOU). There is no need to have an elaborate, legalistic type of

The Action Learning Plan   91

document. However, in a page or two, it should lay out mutual expectations, what the set expects of the client, and what the client expects of the set. If the set needs to manipulate data, the agreement will commonly include the expectation from the set that data be provided promptly (e.g., within 48 hours) upon request. The memorandum of understanding also makes clear what the set will deliver to the client and the limits of the set investigation.

There can be instances when the client will decide that more is wanted than initially envisaged. That can lead to additional demands being placed upon the set. The set cannot keep re-gearing to meet fluctuating expectations of the client, especially when having to stay within the time constraints. In such cases, the memorandum of understanding can keep the client from drifting to a new set of requirements. While the memorandum of understanding needs to be clear in its intentions, it also needs to allow the necessary latitude for clarification of the problem. In effect, a set operates in the contracting phase as a consultant group performing one of the biggest services that any consultant can provide: helping the client better understand the problem being addressed. This clarification can often be done as part of the pre-work before the memorandum of understanding is finalized.

Since the MOU only addresses key bottom line deliverables and conventions governing the action learning set and client relationship, it does not necessarily convey the level of complexity being dealt with. The problem outline and background are usually covered in a separate document.

Because construction of such a memorandum of understanding can be an uncertain task to those contemplating one for the first time, an actual memorandum, modified only to protect confidentiality is shown in Example 4.1 at the end of this chapter. One of the complicating issues in matching the expectations of client and set in a memorandum of understanding is the issue of set composition. The client has to understand that set members, though performing consulting functions, are deliberately being placed in a situation far removed from their customary practice and expertise. That client has to be willing to entertain the idea that the "nonexpert thinking" action learning demands can in fact yield new insights and solution options.

PRECAUTIONS: WHAT CAN GO WRONG?

Listed below are some principal issues that tend to surface as part of the group dynamics of a set and the lessons learned.

Issue/Problem	Lessons Learned
1. Set member tries to take over the group.	• This triggers divisiveness. This is usually countered by the set.
2. Set member does not like working in teams.	• There is a need to adjust/learn team skills. • As a last resort, remove the person from the team.
3. Undercurrent/lingering frictions in sets.	• Bypassing problem or using "band-aids" is usually ineffective. • The set needs to get it out in the open and address it.
4. Inequality of commitment/workload.	• This is unacceptable. • Lying back and letting others "carry you" are not behaviors a high-performing team allows.
5. Imbalance between pursuit of task and attention to learning (reflective component necessary).	• The depth of learning gets short-circuited. • The set needs to make time for the reflective component.
6. Need to meet as a group concurrently (*all* present at all meetings for entire meeting time).	• The only way to sustain continuity flow is to travel together.

The Action Learning Plan

7. Failure to adequately determine group norms through consensus up front.	• This is the number one source of problems in sets. • The set cannot shortcut the group norming process, which does not ever really end.

Tuckman's forming, norming, storming, performing, and adjournment have full applicability to action learning (Tuckman & Jensen, 1977). The group forming and norming steps need to occur. Set members need to fully appreciate where others in the set are coming from. One technique that can be used to help in the formation step is to ask the set members to develop a collective group resume, as they would do if they were part of a consulting company. What are the strengths of the set? What can it collectively bring to the table? This opens up early dialogue. There can be surprises here. It usually leads to identification of assets that far exceed expectations. There also needs to be an opportunity for the group members to get to know each other at a deeply personal level. What concerns do individual set members feel? What do they do well, and what do they not do well?

As part of the norming step, sets are asked to arrive at a working team agreement. What is shown below is an actual agreement developed by an extremely effective action learning set. The end product must be fully owned and agreed to by each set member.

Working Team Agreement

1. Keep any negative comments to a minimum so as to promote a positive learning experience.

2. There will be no gossip or partnering among group members.

3. Exercise professional courtesy toward each other and respect each other's ideas.

4. Take mutual responsibility to stay on task. It is important

to be on time and to use our designated time (maximum of two hours) efficiently.

5. It is very important that each set member be present for all meetings to maintain continuity.
6. We will be understanding toward each other if a conflict arises and a member cannot attend.
7. Each group member gets equal speaking time.
8. Keep a record of process of each meeting. This is done by rotating the job of secretary.
9. Have a secretary take five minutes at the end of each meeting (1) to make sure we are all on the same page; (2) to confirm that we all agree on what has been accomplished; (3) to make sure we all feel comfortable; and (4) to state the goals, plans, roles, and expectations for the following meeting.
10. The conflict resolution protocol is to take a democratic vote.
11. Divide the workflow into categories, such as marketing, data gathering, and so on.
12. Stay focused. Any member of the group should step in to get us back on track.
13. Everything is decided by consensus.
14. Explore all possibilities, with each member voicing an opinion, before implementing a course of action.
15. Air disagreements. Don't leave a meeting with bad feelings.
16. Maintain maximum confidentiality of our client and team members.

The Reflective Component

What does not come across as a discrete area of address in this working team agreement, just highlighted, even though implied, is the issue of reflection. As indicated earlier in the book, this can be very difficult to accomplish. The set becomes driven by the project, and time becomes a very valuable and finite commodity. The reflective component can become a casualty and fall out on the cutting room floor. In our experience, once the value of the reflective component is discovered, sets begin to incorporate it naturally in their process flow.

A major contributor to ensuring that reflection occurs is an agreement to welcome and respect silence. If set members are not talking, they can be responding to inner feelings and insights that they can then share at will. Sets will quickly see the value of this if they establish it as one of their operating guidelines. Spontaneous ways are found to find reflection time, once the importance and joy of it are recognized. In 2001, one set that Dilworth worked with got into the habit of ending its four to six hour meetings on a weekend with a full hour of reflection. They also had periodic breakfast meetings together, where the only agenda item was learning.

Maintenance of a learning log, covering what is learned after each get-together, can be helpful, as well. This self-dialogue can prove very important to the personal growth of the individual. In the 1996 experience in England, alluded to earlier, we recall a participant who wrote in her reflective essay at the end of the experience, that she could hardly wait to get to her room at night to write entries in her log. She said that when she self-imposed this form of introspection, she found herself to be "good company."

Both Dilworth and Willis create "hybrid sets" (not to be confused with the hybrid model for action learning utilized by Willis). Willis asks as many as three sets to meet together and trade insights from their client set activity. This combination of sets works well because all of her students (from 15–18) will have had many earlier classes together and will already have formed high levels of trust as a total group.

In Dilworth's case, hybrid sets are formed by drawing participants from each of the regular joint project sets into new set formations. In effect, individuals from the regular sets are "re-setted" to put them in contact with other set participants. This helps diffuse the sharp project focus. Hybrid sets are encouraged to spend their time focusing only on the learning component, even though that will draw in experience related to the task. Dilworth has found that participants begrudge the time when the concept is outlined; however, once they have been through a dialogue session in a hybrid set, they tend to become advocates. It allows them to break free of what can seem to be the vise-like grip of the project being pursued. Some genuine collective reflection is the result.

We require students involved with the action learning experience in our courses, always related to a real problem of complexity, to submit an essay reflecting on the experience. Both of us use a set of critical incidents to help guide students in their critical reflection. Participants are encouraged to address the same critical incidents when making entries in their learning logs. Critical incidents include (but are not confined to):

- When were you most engaged?
- When were you most distanced?
- When were you most puzzled?
- When did you feel most affirmed?
- What gaps did you identify in your learning, and what will be your personal learning strategies for closing them?

One other tool to promote critical reflection is now in use, a version of the Global Team Process Questionnaire (GTPQ) developed by ITAP International in Princeton, New Jersey. A modified version of the GTPQ has been developed by ITAP International in collaboration with Dilworth for action learning sets, called the Action Learning Team Process Questionnaire (ALTPQ). The ALTPQ has 25 Likert-scaled questions; one question related to identification of barriers to team work; and an opportunity to list the top four positive and four top negative things about the action learning experience. The Likert-scale questions cover a wide range, including distribution of work (relative equality), clarity of set agenda, clarity of set member roles, effectiveness of the set (as a team), quality of communication within the set, level of trust, and level of support being provided by those external to the set.

Each set member scores the questionnaire privately. It is then analyzed electronically, with each set receiving a profile of questionnaire results by question. Set members were, of course, providing their perceptions when they completed the questionnaire. The matrix profile provided immediately identifies areas of broad variance, such as four of five set members ranking the quality of communication in the set at the top of the scale, whereas one member ranks it at the bottom. The collective review of the matrix profile and reactions to action learning (positive and negative) tend to fuel comprehensive discussions in the set. The ALTPQ results not only leverage in-depth group reflection but also allow the set to consider how it needs to modify the group dynamics. How can trust level be improved? It can also lead to a revisit of the working team agreement.

You cannot trigger the action learning process and then put learning on "automatic pilot." While we serve as learning coaches, we purposely avoid intervening in set business because we hurt the process. However, there are other forms of intervention that we believe are necessary. One form of intervention is nurturing support of the learners, as a mentor and good listener. Action learning, because it can open up self-doubt and cause rethinking of the assumptions one has held dear, needs support systems. We invite interaction with the participants in helping them address what they view as personal problem points in their lives. In Chapter 7, "The Transformative Potential of Action Learning," we offer evidence that many individuals who undertake action learning also find that it has changed some of their fundamental belief systems. Their essays tell us they are surprised and pleased with these results.

SUMMARY

There can be a number of things going on concurrently in an action learning initiative. For example, you can end up developing set composition at the same time that work is proceeding to establish a working agreement with a client to sponsor the action learning experience. There can even be some preliminary diagnoses by the learning coach in making sure that problems being identified for resolution are at an appropriate level of difficulty and capable of being dealt with in the time allotted.

Action learning set composition is a critical step. The quality of the learning to be realized tends to be in direct proportion to the artfulness of set engineering. The fundamental goal is to build in diversity in providing for a variety of perspectives.

The action learning model you select will also influence the quality of learning. We believe that the joint project model has inherent advantages over the EBO model for the reasons that have been enumerated. Selection of the right project and having a clear understanding with the client can be make or break issues. A memorandum of understanding between the client and the action learning set is essential.

Finally, it is important that the group dynamics receive careful address up front, especially the group formation and group norming stages. This needs to be a solid platform. Negotiating a working team agreement among set members is strongly recommended. Action learning sets can display haste in moving through the norming process, only to find out later, when the pressure of the project effort is most intense, that the norming process was flawed. The best advice on norming is to realize that it is never over. This area needs to be revisited regularly.

Example 4.1
Memorandum of Understanding
Between
Greenway Construction Company
And
Action Learning Set B

Greenway Construction Company requires assistance in designing a recruitment program to include the selection, training, retention, and orientation of new employees for a new start-up company. The new work encompasses areas not dealt with previously, including an assembly line that is to be up and operating as quickly as possible. Project time is urgent. This in effect constitutes development of HR strategies leading to rapid assembly of a workforce possessing the necessary mix of competencies.

I. **Parties.**

The document constitutes an agreement between Greenway Construction Company and Action Learning Set B, consisting of James Smith, Mary Whipple, Jean Ramsey, Fred Magnum, and Betty Sue Lloyd.

II. **Purpose.**

A. *Background.* Greenway Construction undertakes this project as part of an action learning program of which Action Learning Set B is a part.

B. *Project.* Action Learning Set B will assist Greenway Construction Company in creating profiles for positions as well as the processes for recruiting, selecting, and training of new employees for the new Ridgefield plant of the company. Additionally, Action Learning Set B will construct an incentive plan for the operation.

III. **Mutual Interest of the Parties.**

Both parties have a vested interest in the success of the

project. Cooperation is expected by both parties to see the project to fruition.

IV. **Responsibilities of the Parties.**
   A. Action Learning Set B. Conditions of satisfaction—per our site visit, the following are the perceived conditions for satisfaction.
      1. Develop job descriptions for Greenway Construction Company specific to the Ridgefield plant, based on required skills for the following positions, as discussed.
         —Welding
         —Inspector
         —Assembler
         —Inventory control specialist
         —Crane operator
         —Transportation coordinator
      2. Match developed job descriptions with those in use elsewhere in the company, as well as any best practice examples that can be identified.
      3. Develop a recruitment selection and hiring plan.
      4. Develop an orientation/training program, making recommendations, as needed.
      5. Provide recommendations to incorporate teamwork into the workflow.
      6. Develop an incentive plan to retain employees.
   B. Greenway Construction Company
      1. Participate jointly in the project.
      2. Provide information within 24–48 hours from date and time of request whenever possible. Notify Action Learning Set B if unable to provide information within the stated timeframe.
      3. Provide expertise and advice on existing process functions.
      4. Provide general oversight of activities conducted pursuant to this requirement.

V. **Period of Agreement and Modification/Termination.**

Action Learning Group B promises to deliver a final report and presentation to Greenway Construction Company the week of April 30, 2001. Affiliation between the stated parties will conclude at that time.

This memorandum is dated February 15, 2001.

CHAPTER 5

Phases of the Action Learning Cycle

No organization is likely to embrace action learning unless there is some person within it ready to fight on its behalf. Careful observation suggests that it is rarely a conviction about the merits of action learning as such that first inclines people to take it up; only when they become convinced that their existing approaches to managerial and supervisory training are not likely to get anywhere will they turn to the untried and the challenging. Since the last persons to admit that existing development schemes fall below desirable standards are those who run them, it is rare for the active motivation to start with the personnel department, or with the chief training officer, who probably owes his present seniority to having built up a system now under attack. His instincts are to jump to its defense; one way to disparage whatever challenges it, and when action learning is imperfectly understood, it can very quickly be disparaged.
—Reginald W. Revans (1983, pp. 71–72)

What is usually missing in writings on action learning is a clear expression of how the various parts of action learning interrelate. Listing of techniques, in and of itself, does not give you as the learning coach a picture of the ebb and flow of an action learning experience. How do you deal with a client? What advice do you give set members for handling client-related problems? What rules of confidentiality need to be in place? What do you do about conflicts that arise in sets? What kind of preliminary information on action learning do the learners need to be exposed to beforehand if they are to be successful? How do you deal with the stress generated by project pressure within

Phases of the Action Learning Cycle

the sets? Whenever you deal with real world issues of urgency within set time constraints, there will be stress and it can be significant. That stress is more likely to occur in joint problem sets, where the issue can be extremely difficult and demanding, in part because of the need for effective teamwork within the set to be successful. In Everyone Bring One (EBO) sets, the pressure will tend to be less. There is less vesting in a common purpose.

How do you build self-confidence in those who do not feel up to the task? What are reasonable expectations regarding client behavior and what occurs within the set itself? How do you go about promoting empowerment? Some have only operated in command and control environments, where the opportunity for independent action is minimal. We have had action learning participants ask: "When are you going to tell us what to do?" Some only seem comfortable operating within tight guidelines. When they are "set free" to manage their own effort and learning in a set, they may try to create surrogate leaders in the set who will tell them what to do. Usually, that can be reversed and the learner weaned from a dependency orientation. What is the role of a learning coach, and how does it need to be modified to fit the circumstances?

What this chapter sets out to do is systematically walk through the action learning process, providing an integrated look at what can reasonably be expected to occur and how you counter the problems that arise. Let's take another look at the initiation phase and describe each part of the cycle in turn.

THE INITIATION PHASE

This aspect of action learning deserves more thoughtful attention than it often gets. Contexts and culture should be clearly on the mind of anyone entering the initiation phase of a potential action learning program. A second part of the initiation requires some fairly intense engagement with the problem statement(s), working to clarify what they mean and in many cases helping to restate them. Who is "the real client"? And what does this client expect? At some end point, you as the learning coach

INITIATION PHASE

Learning coach shows intent to employ action learning.

Learning coach considers specific context.

Learning coach scopes and understands organizational culture.

Learning coach gains top management support.

Learning coach identifies initial problem statement(s) with prospective client.

Learning coach determines specific client(s) and client expectations and arrives at refined problem statements.

Learning coach decides whether or not to go forward.

Figure 5.1 Activities in the Initiation Phase

need to make a decision as to whether this particular project should proceed. It is time to consider these elements of initiation in more detail (Figure 5.1).

Learning Coach Considers Specific Context

Dealing with a hospital can be different from dealing with a correctional facility, public school faculty, or a state transportation agency. The specific contexts are quite different. For example, you will be dealing with a widely dispersed employee population in a state transportation agency. That will influence what you can reasonably expect to do if the program is to extend to line workers. The correctional facility setting will usually have some common denominators that need to be kept in mind. The systems will tend to be so highly controlled, because of regulatory requirements and the clientele served, that opportunities to use action learning in a correctional facility may prove minimal. Since action learning encourages people to take control of their own lives and question the status quo, this can seem entirely out of place in a correctional institution. Inmates are not expected to question the rules of governance set forth by the warden and the government. On the other hand, when you extend the context to the upper echelons of the correctional system, at a state, regional, or national level, the opportunities to have meaningful action learning experiences can increase.

The business context varies according to size of the business. Action learning can fit well with small business, but it can be difficult to support based on the lack of internal resources, including expertise. In larger businesses, the issue becomes subcontexts. For example, within GE you have major corporate segments dealing with aircraft engines, the entertainment industry, financial systems and products (GE Capital), medical services, locomotives, aircraft engines, and plastics. Each subcontext has different characteristics. As we have all learned intuitively in dealing with various enterprises, there are certain characteristics we associate with a type of enterprise. Banking as a context will tend to be ultraconservative. The military will tend to be rigid. Public school systems have their own rigidities and can be very difficult to change.

We are not talking about an elaborate analytical process you need to go through in examining a context. There simply needs to be an appreciation that context counts. We have seen situations where there is an assumption that the same kind of action learning programs and patterns fit anywhere. While action learning can, in fact, work just about anywhere, including internationally, you need to stop and consider context and its broad implications.

Learning Coach Scopes and Understands Organizational Culture

A distinction needs to be drawn between climate and culture. Climate is more fleeting and particularly sensitive to the leadership in place at the time. It includes practices, policies, and procedures. Culture relates to the underlying belief systems, and they can be developed over a period of years. One thinks of IBM, which, for many years, was said to operate in the shadow of Tom Watson, its founder, because of the powerful stamp he placed on the company.

In 2001, and going on for over a year, you see a battle between climate and culture in Hewlett-Packard, under the leadership of its new chief executive officer, Carly Fiorina. She has the unenviable role of trying to change a culture with dysfunctional characteristics in today's environment. This involves trying to change a deeply embedded culture that is extraordinarily change resistant. The climate has changed dramatically in a year through major restructuring and fundamental changes in long-standing policies and practices, but the underlying culture is changing very slowly. The conflict has been even more evident in the intense debate ongoing in 2002 on whether to merge Hewlett-Packard with Compaq. Hewlett-Packard has been described as a "plodding culture" (Nee, 2001, p. 115).

The main point of the discussion is that the climate cannot be used as the sole gauge of how to adapt action learning to the organization. As indicated in the example early in the book, when the CEO of the company decided he really did not want to empower his people, surface impressions related to climate masked the true situation. One of us had a recent experience with action learning in a major company. Going in, everything seemed perfect. There was high-level support in the company, the clients (multiple) seemed committed to change, and they were perfect hosts. As things turned out, the culture had a darker side and really was not that interested in real change. In many respects, the hard work that went into the action learning effort seemed for naught. However, the learners maintained their perspective and rated their involvement as an extremely beneficial experience. They had become much more perceptive in understanding the dynamics of organizational culture.

In the end, it is not easy to decipher a corporate culture but there are ways you can speed the process; one way is to go to people you know in the company and have them interpret the culture. That person needs to come from the specific organization where action learning is to be introduced. You don't go to any GE employee, for example, for a reading on the culture of NBC (a subpiece of GE). The best advice is to get inside the company to the extent possible, observe the environment, and talk with people.

Why do you want to understand the culture? You need to know whether it is a culture that is supportive of change. Is it a trustful climate? Dilworth remembers a true situation in the mid-1990s when a group of employees were called together in the morning and told that a significant number of them would be subject to downsizing. The same afternoon, many of the same employees were called back together again and informed that a quality initiative was being launched, and if they wanted to keep their jobs, they had better support it. That is obviously not the kind of culture in which you want to try and introduce action learning. A climate of fear is not conducive to action learning, or any other positive change initiative for that matter.

In some cases, in considering action learning on a large scale, like GE, you need to work with the culture before introducing action learning. There may be a need, for example, to better open up communication.

An example here, perhaps, makes the point best. If you are going to plant a crop and expect it to grow, do you plant it in well-cultivated soil, or, do you plant it in a desert environment, characterized by parched earth? The question is an easy one to answer, and yet interventions like action learning can be introduced in a desert-like environment, then surprise can be expressed when there is no real crop at all, or it is subject to stunted growth. Quite often the methodology is blamed, whether it is action learning, an organization development (OD) strategy, or a quality management initiative.

It is not a matter of seeking out the most perfect culture in which to apply action learning. You simply need to have done a decent assessment of the culture before you decide to go forward with an action learning program, and then you need to engineer your action learning design to fit the circumstances. A truism here is that you can be considering use of action learning in your own culture and not really understand that culture. We do not usually look through a lens labeled corporate culture in our own organization any more than we necessarily give attention to the U.S. culture as citizens of the United States. You need to do some critical examination and reflection in such cases.

Learning Coach Gains Top Management Support

You may be dealing with a clash of paradigms when you approach top management. Their world centers on the bottom line and the next quarterly report. That is not meant to be pejorative. That is simply the reality. They are not going to sit still for any elaborate run through or testimonial about action learning. The interest is in performance, productivity and business results (translate that to a better profit and loss statement, and enlargement of market share). When they take a serious look at action learning is after the results come in. Therefore, it does not usually pay to discuss action learning in depth when you approach the top managers. That doesn't mean that you disguise the fact that action learning is involved, or fail to outline some of the rudimentary principles, but the real focus needs to be on the issue/problem to be addressed and what the consulting group is to focus on and resolve. That needs to be the true start point. The reflective component is what the learning coach helps reinforce with the action learning set alongside of the work activity related to the task.

You need to specify the uniqueness of the team, the fact that it is a low-cost/no-cost intervention, and that the action learning set is committed to work with the problem with the intent of solving it. In turn, the client is to provide the necessary support, whether it is resources or information, in a timely manner.

There has to be a feeling in the end between the learning coach and top managers that it can be a good partnership. There is no specific yardstick that you can use. It is a gut feeling and it is based on your perceptions of what is there. How does the mosaic fit together? As indicated earlier, it is more than understanding top management—as important as it is—you need to get inside the culture. You need to listen to top management and then see if what they told you is reflected in the culture. Top management can view their organization through rose-colored glasses.

Learning Coach Identifies Initial Problem Statement with Prospective Client

Identifying the problem statement is not necessarily as easy as it may seem. As Revans's Belgian example teaches us, the problem can be quite different than that surmised at the outset. Failure to move alloy steel in large enough quantities was the tip of the iceberg. It ultimately led to the real problem, and it had nothing to do with the production of alloy steel. The problem was rooted in the compensation system. It is a rarity when the initial problem statement presented by the client does not undergo some form of modification. In some respects, they may be too close to the problem. One can surmise that this was a factor in the Belgian case. As noted earlier, one of the most important services one can provide to the business—and it can occur up front—is in the clarification of the problem. The learning coach works to achieve problem clarification with the client, in making sure that it is a coherent problem, and that it is complex and worthy of examination via action learning. This helps you get to a go/no-go on whether to strike a preliminary agreement to collaborate.

After the set initiates direct negotiations with the client, with the learning coach as a go-between and facilitator, the problem statement may further change shape. During this period, preliminary to consummation of a written agreement, the action learning set begins its learning process and, in effect, promotes the learning process of the client by asking thought-provoking questions, among them, the System Alpha related questions: What is happening? What ought to be happening? How do you make it happen? This serves to get everything on firm ground *or* leads you to determine that it will not be worthwhile working with the client.

Dilworth met with one of the largest federal agencies in 2000, seeking a viable action learning project. It was quickly determined that it was not a worthwhile project. They were not truly after real change. The problem was more administrative than substantive and the culture would have been extremely difficult to work with.

It is extremely important to review proposed projects carefully. Is the client really interested in doing it? Is there a sense of urgency? Is the problem a viable one and thus far unsolved? Is the culture likely to be receptive to recommendations that represent significant change? Will the client fully support the efforts of the set, including timely provision of information?

Learning Coach Determines Specific Client(s) and Their Expectations

Determination of the client is a process that needs to be painstakingly worked through. The person you initially coordinate with in the organization may not be the real client. It is also often a case of multiple clients rather than a single one. In the case of multiple clients, there will usually be a primary one, or a client that is first among equals.

A good way to sort through this is to ask your contact in the company: Who will be making the decisions on recommendations the action learning set proposes? Who will be accountable for implementing the decisions? You can end up with interesting answers to such questions and they can lead to other questions. If person A has responsibility for the decisions and persons B, C, and D must implement them, will they accept the decisions reached by A? In 2001, an action learning set Dilworth was involved with discovered that the decision maker (person A) had less authority over other managers than had been conveyed.

Phases of the Action Learning Cycle 111

It scrambled the ability to get timely input in response to action learning set requests for data. Since an overall process was being examined, and some of the supporting players would not provide data, it was not possible to deliver the products in the comprehensive way the client (person A) had requested.

What can make client scoping devilishly hard is that you are largely dependent on good faith. If a client sits in what appears to be the requisite position of authority on the organizational chart, and promises to deliver on all aspects of the agreement, there is a limit to what you can do to check veracity. It underscores the need to check with alternative sources whenever possible before striking an agreement.

We can think of one instance when a client intentionally deceived the learning coach and action learning set. He had asked that action learning be used to assess the strategies of the private association he was with as executive director in a changing marketplace. It was a very exciting project, since the survival of the association was in jeopardy. Two months into the agreement, the client admitted that he never really had any intention of going forward with the project. He had decided to leave the organization and become a consultant. If he had not accepted the action learning project arrangement, he might have tipped his hand to the organization prematurely regarding his intentions to resign. He did provide an option. The action learning set could work with him in his consultancy status and then sell the solution to the association. This was clearly unethical behavior in several respects. The action learning set was immediately withdrawn and assigned an alternative project elsewhere. There is a saying that "anything can happen in real estate." The same can probably be said about action learning.

Learning Coach Decides Whether to go Forward

In the end, it is a subjective call, but optimally, with the support of as many facts as can be brought to bear. It becomes a matter of testing the client's reliability and viability of the project, to the extent you can. You also need to match the people you are bringing together in the set to work on the problem with their intellectual ability to realistically tackle the problem. While the problem will often be by design an unfamiliar one, you need to make sure that the set members are up to the rigor of what is to occur in terms of educational level, sophistication, and prior managerial experience.

THE ACTION LEARNING PHASE

Some aspects of this phase have already been addressed with respect to determination of an appropriate action learning model and determination of set composition. Here the entire action learning phase unfolds (Figure 5.2).

Learning Coach Determines Appropriate Action Learning Model

As indicated in Chapter 4, there are two basic models, plus the Belgian model and the hybrid variation that Willis uses. There are also offshoots of the models that can be considered. For example, the Everyone Bring Your Own (EBO) model does not necessarily mean that set members pick their own projects. There can be some form of screening process and supporting criteria, in making sure that projects are truly worthy. You could even apply a modified version of the Belgian model, with set members each to be given a project from his or her own overall organization (e.g., GE), but from a suborganization other than their own. This requires much more advance work than the basic EBO model.

You might also choose to go with a joint project but purposely seed the set with one or two people who will be on the implementation team (or action learning set) once decisions are reached on how to move toward solution of the actual problem. This allows you to bring in people who have the requisite expertise to manage the implementation phase. As mentioned in Chapter 4, this has its downside. It can turn off the impetus to

ACTION LEARNING PHASE

Learning coach determines appropriate action learning model.

Learning coach determines set composition.

Learning coach familiarizes participants with process.

Set forms and norms, arriving at conventions to govern group dynamics.

Set examines advance material from client, including problem statement(s). The focus is on Q.
- What's happening?
- What needs to happen?
- How do they make it happen?

Set meets with client and determines mutual expectations and timetable.

Set conducts field research and collects data. Set refines and develops P as necessary.

Set analyzes data and arrives at recommendations.

Figure 5.2 Activities in the Action Learning Phase

ask fresh questions. There is another downside as well. What if the problem with alloy steel, outlined in Chapter 4, had been dealt with as a joint problem and seeded with a couple of alloy steel experts? In this case, you would have found that the action learning set charged with implementation really needed compensation expertise. However, you did not know that until you had fully worked the problem. To have seeded the set with a couple of alloy steel experts might have injected the kind of P that would have caused the set to travel down the wrong roads in identifying the problem.

Learning Coach Determines Set Composition

Remember that this is more art than science. Review it from a number of angles, *and* in relation to the action learning model you have selected. As indicated in Chapter 4, your usual goal is to build in as much diversity as possible, in order to bring as many perspectives to the table as possible. You look at personality, gender, ethnicity, background, learning styles, educational foundations and any other factors deemed helpful.

What you want to avoid doing is creating cliques, where the set becomes a social club. Both of us have seen situations where a pool of people was allowed to self-select their sets. This seems democratic enough, but it also has a predictable outcome. Those of like mind band together, thus shutting down (or at least reducing) the ability to entertain and act on different points of view.

Learning Coach Familiarizes Participants with Process

This puts you in another "trick box." How much do they need to know ahead of time? If you give them too much information, you can become a merchant for P. On the other hand, they need to know some of the basics and how the process of critical reflection can be fully realized.

Two real-life examples will be provided. In preparation for the program in England in 1996, alluded to earlier in the book,

Phases of the Action Learning Cycle 115

the following was done one month *before* the participants arrived in England from the United States, Canada, and Australia: (1) Participants each received a binder of material with various selected readings in action learning and (2) they received a second volume containing profile information on each participant (a one-page autobiographical statement, an indication of prior experience with action learning, and the person's expectations for the two-week concentrated program). The second volume also provided an indication of the set they were in, names and contact information on set members, and a statement of the joint problem the set was to address. Agenda information and administrative material were also a part of this volume. In the process just described, set members were encouraged to make advance contact with their fellow set members by telephone or e-mail.

At the kick-off session in England, with all five sets convened, only 30 minutes was devoted to a summary overview of the program. Sets then split off and met for an hour to discuss the problem they had been given and to start the group norming process. Following that, all sets climbed on buses and went for their initial meeting with their respective clients, all in the health care field. This was a case of throwing them into the deep end of the pool. In the end, the process worked, and the group came away feeling tightly bonded for the most part. They had faced up to a major challenge together. You could call this action learning's version of a Marine Corps boot camp. There were some extraordinary outcomes from this experience as reported by the learners. This will be referenced in Chapter 7, "The Transformative Potential of Action Learning."

The second example is a more customary approach to front-end familiarization of learners with the action learning process. Both of us, working with sets in a higher education setting, allow set members three weeks for gaining some familiarity with action learning and going through a group norming process, including arriving at the working team agreement—how they will go about interacting with one another. This is a "get to know each other" phase, with some of the time taken up by discussion of the assigned joint project.

In the fourth and fifth weeks of Dilworth's classes, sets

spend time on site with the client in working through a memorandum of agreement. The learning coach accompanies them as essentially a silent partner. Both Dilworth and Willis invite client managers to present the proposed problems to the entire class, so that each set knows what other sets will be working on. The purpose is to establish a sense among clients that they are not alone in this strange undertaking, and that other client organizations are putting themselves on the line with action learning projects, also. After presentation of the problems, Willis asks each client manager to go to a break room with the set members assigned to that manager, and the group makes arrangements for all subsequent meetings, usually after working hours, at the client site. From the very beginning, clients understand themselves to be a part of the action learning set and they make the commitment to keep the set meetings on their calendars unless called away by emergencies.

Part of the introductory orientation before meeting the managers is on control of stress, since set members can expect to experience it. The learning coach also strives to create a supportive environment. The sets are encouraged to consider how they will deal with conflict resolution in their working team agreements.

We normally use little advance reading material in setting up the action learning experience, nor do we do an extensive elaboration of group dynamics and conflict resolution. We give the sets some foundation in these areas, but dealing with the issues is part of the learning process for action learning participants. There is only so much you can learn out of a book about group dynamics and conflict resolution. Every situation is a bit different. You learn by having to work through such situations.

Set Forms and Norms

The act of forming starts the action learning process. The act of norming never really ends. It needs to be revisited along the way. There is a problem that often occurs during the group norming process, even when you caution action learning sets to avoid it. A better way to describe it is as a trap into which action learning sets fall because of initial good feelings. Because set members like each other and feel comfortable working together, they believe that going through a full-blown norming process is unnecessary. They cannot see themselves ever storming. In their view, they will move directly from forming to performing, no need to go through Tuckman's norming and storming. Later, they may be hit by a violent squall as the pressure to deliver results mounts in relation to time.

In our experience, action learning sets respond one of two ways when such squall lines develop. The first is to take heed, stopping long enough to do some effective group process review and norming. This is the wise course. The second response is a conscious decision to muddle through and try to mask the conflict. "We are pretty close to the end. Let's just try and keep tempers in check and move on!" The latter course of action in our experience can lead to serious problems. Rather than being ameliorated, the underlying problems tend to get exacerbated as the pressures related to project completion build. Willis recalls a case in which racial tensions began to impact progress. The two students made a pact between themselves to resolve the conflict privately before the next set meeting. They did so, and it was only after the set experiences were over that their learning coach learned of the problem. Dilworth can recall two instances when the internal conflict within a set became so severe that the differences could not be resolved. In both cases, a set member had to be removed at the behest of the other set members. This is rare, but it underscores the need to work through the norming process fully at the outset, and then regularly revisit/tend to it.

Set Examines Advance Material from Client

As noted earlier, this is an important step. If the learning coach has properly scoped the client organization and problem statement, the problem should be a reasonably clear representation of the client's concerns. However, the first real work of the set is to make sure that the problem statement is fully understood by all hands. This, in turn, becomes the basis for determining what the client expects, and what the set should expect from the client. In the case of Willis's students, the client is meeting with the set, and clarification is arrived at in the course of continuing discussions. The set uses the System Alpha questions to probe and further their understanding: What is happening? What needs to happen? How do you go about making it happen?

Set Meets with Client and Determines Mutual Expectations and Timetable

The initial meeting(s) with the client should lead to a memorandum of understanding, as noted in Chapter 4, that clearly articulates what each party is responsible for doing. In our experience, nothing is more important to the client-set relationship than this memorandum of understanding. It provides a basis for getting things back on track when one of the parties fails to deliver on their part of the bargain. This aspect of the action learning process should not be rushed. If it is not an accurate reflection of mutual expectations, it is likely to lead to misunderstandings later. This is especially true if the client is not a part of the set and can easily prioritize their work in ways that fail to support set activity.

One important aspect of the agreement is the protection of confidentiality. The set will be operating with sensitive client information. In some instances the client will ask that nondisclosure statements be signed by each set member and the learning coach.

The next steps resemble most closely the scientific method, and Revans labels this System Beta.

Set Conducts Field Research and Collects Data

This can be a sizable task and requires close coordination with the client organization in making sure that interviewees (as appropriate) are available in the timeframe necessary. It also requires that organizational data be turned over to the action learning set in a timely manner. The set should have a clear idea of how it will organize and analyze data collected. This process is certainly more collaborative if the client is a member of the set.

Set Analyzes Data and Arrives at Recommendations

This step includes getting ready for the formal presentation of the findings and recommendations to the client. It requires rehearsal in order to properly organize the message and stay within time constraints. The immediate client will have a reasonably good idea what will be contained in the presentation if they have been a member of the set, but in Willis's experience, the set members put in extra hours without the client present and there are always additional insights, further detail, and further enlightenment for that client.

There is a trap here that action learning sets need to avoid. The set needs to know who in the organization will be in the audience when findings and recommendations are presented. There can be a tendency to prepare the presentation with only the immediate clients in mind. However, the audience almost always extends beyond the immediate clients. There may be senior members of the organization present, for whom the immediate clients work. There may also be people in attendance who will need to implement any recommendations. It therefore becomes imperative that the set provide the full story, and not shortcut it in the belief that those in the audience already know about the project and have full particulars. That is a dangerous assumption. The final presentation needs to be engineered so that it does not talk past anyone. The written report should be similarly engineered. If there is a sincere interest in having the findings given full attention and recommendations implemented, then they must be presented in a way that facilitates complete understanding of the genesis of the project, what was to be delivered, agreement between the client and action learning set on outcomes, the recommendations, *and* a notion of how implementation of recommendations can be brought to fruition.

IMPLEMENTATION PHASE

This phase is what everyone has been waiting for: client, set members, and learning coach alike (Figure 5.3). Everyone experiences a mood of anticipation tinged with anxiety, like rehearsing for opening night at the theater and then performing for a first night audience. While there are predictable preparations, no one is absolutely certain what will happen.

Set Presents Results

This is the moment for presenting the sorted findings and making recommendations to the client. Sometimes there is even need to suggest "red flags" that management needs to be particularly concerned about. Preparing, delivering, listening, and responding to findings constitute intense learning experiences. If the client has chosen to include others who have not been involved up to this point, the tension mounts. Our experience has been, however, that it tends to resolve itself positively. Nothing is "cut and dried" about this event.

But the presentation is only the beginning. If there is a phase related to action learning that tends to be somewhat murky and uncharted, it is the implementation phase. In the Everyone Bring One (EBO) model, the trail seems to end with the expectation that the recommendations of the set members will be adopted and implemented.

The joint action learning model can also lack linkages between the presentation of findings and recommendations and what happens thereafter. In GE, they have rather precise follow-up mechanisms, because the credibility of the work-outs would decline rapidly if there was a sense that the decisions made were somewhat artificial and not subject to follow up.

The issue becomes what general process of implementation should be in place. The following steps represent our views on how to model the implementation.

IMPLEMENTATION PHASE

Set presents results to client orally and in writing.

↓

Set assists client in transitioning to implementation phase.
- Helps those to implement understand findings and develop plan of attack
- Promotes buy-in by those to implement

↓

Set reflects on learning that has occurred.
- What do members know that they didn't before?
- How would they do it differently next time?
- How has the experience changed their belief systems?
- What were the shortfalls in personal knowledge and how can this be fixed?
- After a review of the learning process, how can they apply it professionally, organizationally, and personally in the future?

↓

Set is available to assist in clarifying solution options.

↓

Internal implementation team/set sees project through to completion.

↓

Management evaluates outcomes in relation to their expectations.

Figure 5.3 Activities in the Implementation Phase

Set Assists Client in Transitioning to the Implementation Phase

This assumes that a follow-on set will be established by the client to handle implementation of recommendations. Since members of a joint set (if you follow Revans' philosophy) are ideally drawn from areas not related to the problem under review, it seems logical to assume that the expertise to implement would need to exist in the follow-on set. We firmly believe there needs to be such a follow-on apparatus. It tends to resemble the follow-on architecture in the Belgian model.

The follow-on set's ability to accomplish implementation successfully will depend on buy in *and* knowing the full particulars of how the problem was analyzed and recommendations arrived at. The best way to do this may be to seed the follow-on set with two members of the initial problem-scoping set. The best formula is probably to establish a four- or five-person follow-on set, to which you add two of the initial set members (for a total of six to seven members). The follow-on set should have enlisted "those who know" and "those who can," and certainly, "those who care." The people from the initial set would fall in the "those who care" category.

The kind of linkage just described can go a long way toward exacting full value from the action learning experience. It also can help solve the riddle of handling the implementation when none of the members of the initial set may be familiar with the more technical aspects of the problem they addressed. Willis notes that the follow-on process is more readily assured if the client has been a part of the set activity from the beginning and is "problem owner" from start to finish. This obviously takes a person who cares not only about the implementation, but also about the process to be followed during implementation.

It would appear that in a number of instances, action learning design can push to the side the unfamiliar-unfamiliar dimension that Revans feels is central to action learning. Instead, the typical design opts for placing in the action learning set individuals who are familiar with the area under investigation and can therefore stream forward in dealing with the implementation as well. We think the linkage of the initial set with a follow-on set, as was done by Revans in the Belgian model, comes closest to being the right approach. It is, admittedly, more time consuming to bring together, but the ultimate rewards seem to justify it. The ability to find a solution to the problem can be enhanced—if you believe as we do that there is merit in inducing fresh thinking and causing underlying assumptions to be called into question. We also believe it comes close to Lewin's emphasis on "unfreezing," as the first step of his philosophy of change. In action learning you have two targets of change, the organization and the learners in the action learning set. You are unlikely to unfreeze thinking and get to change if you remain within your normal (and probably very comfortable) paradigm.

Set Reflects on Learning That Has Occurred

While you should be taking stock of learning all along the path, a deep reflection seems best placed after you have moved through the final presentation and are beginning the implementation. Here you can look back at the experience from the start through the final presentation, and now the beginning of the follow-on implementation.

The questions must extend well beyond what went well, and what did not go so well with the project. *The primary reflection must center on what learning has occurred, not on the project.* This means asking the right questions such as:

- What do I know now that I did not know before?
- How have my beliefs (underlying assumptions) changed?
- What have I learned about operating in teams?
- What gaps have I identified in my learning, and what personal learning strategies will I use to narrow or close these gaps?
- How have I changed as a person?

Set Is Available to Assist in Clarifying Solution Options

While we recommend embedding one or two members of the initial set in a follow-on set, there is also a need to have the other members of the initial set available to lend a hand in clarifying options to the extent possible.

Internal Implementation Team/Set Sees Project Through to Completion

This flows out of what has been outlined in relation to earlier steps and needs no further explanation.

Management Evaluates Outcomes in Relation to Their Expectations

It is not sufficient for management to simply take a snapshot after set recommendations are made, and perhaps assume the rest will travel to pocket. There needs to be a timeline for implementation, culminating in a comprehensive review, taking stock of what really happened. Ideally, this should bring the initial set and follow-on set together for final dialogue. A great deal of learning can result from this form of review. It can allow the organization to fine tune its project-related processes, as well as learn how to best employ action learning.

While not mentioned thus far, it seems implicit in the kind of model we have laid out for the implementation phase that attention needs to be given to the reflective component in the case of the implementation set as well as the initial set. This is important learning that needs to be harvested for the benefit of the organization and the individual learners. When the client has been a set member and becomes also part of a follow-on set, there will be a strong advocate for such a harvest.

SUMMARY

You must focus on the flow and how the various pieces of the process interrelate. You need a total systems perspective. It needs to range from the initial stage of the decision to use action learning through the final stage of the implementation. Learning needs to be harvested across the spectrum, meaning that every effort needs to be made to embed reflection as the essential companion piece of action. Learning needs to be kept in focus throughout the entire process, lest things drift into a task force oriented race for project completion that loses track of the fundamental and primary goal of action learning—learning, itself!

CHAPTER 6

Action Learning in Various Domains, Contexts, and Cultures

Although in the past organizations have generally devoted much the greatest part of their development focus to formal learning programs, the bulk of the research to date seems to show that most individual learning in organizations occurs elsewhere, in informal processes of everyday work. Of the estimates that have been attempted, none we have seen places the proportion of learning that comes from formal training or education at more than 20 percent. . . .

—Canadian Centre for Management
Report No. 1, *Continuous Learning*
(1994, p. 16)

In Chapter 2, the various domains and contexts in which action learning can occur were outlined. Throughout the book we have pointed out that while action learning has some universal properties, it needs to be adapted to the context and particular organizational culture, if the initial intervention is to be successful and the action learning program sustained over time. A number of barriers to action learning have been discussed, including a bias that suggests learning and curriculum are indivisible (Chapter 2), a belief system that by definition rules out action learning as an acceptable learning strategy. For this reason, among many, we emphasize in Chapter 3 the need to carefully access the context in which action learning is to be introduced. To overcome barriers, you first need to understand them.

What makes this book different is that it devotes attention

to how you go about employing action learning in various contexts. Most books on the subject devote almost exclusive attention to the business setting. How does employment of action learning differ by context? What can work against you? Based on the times in which we live and the challenges that confront us in the different contexts, what opportunities exist to address the challenges via action learning? Even more importantly, how do we organize the effort to overcome common obstacles and move the program forward? We want you to have some solid handholds in climbing what can be a steep slope.

This chapter will move through each domain and context, in turn, providing a specific understanding of what seem to be the principal opportunities for dealing with challenges that can be in evidence. Where we can point to best practices, we will. However, much of the territory remains unmapped. New economy businesses involving the Internet, for example, have essentially not been addressed yet in terms of potential for action learning. In some cases, we even feel that the way that on line learning programs are designed matches poorly with learning theory. The federal government has occasionally ventured into the use of action learning programs, but it has been very limited. As one final example of unmapped territory, there is little evidence of action learning in the community college setting. We feel that what follows in this chapter will in part involve walking through virgin wilderness, with trails far and few between.

Address of each context will begin with a form of force field analysis (cited in Weisbord, 1987, pp. 73–74), drawing from Lewin's approach in laying out "driving forces" (facilitators) and "restraining forces" (barriers, inhibitors). Earlier, we explored the role that assumptions about the nature and purposes of learning can play in willingness to adopt action learning in any given context. We also speculated about the distribution of four common, discipline-oriented assumptions in five practice domains. Here we acknowledge additional individual and organizational influences, including how the organizations are staffed and structured. Bearing all of these in mind, we provide an amplified index to forces influencing introduction of action learning by domain and specific context.

ACADEMIC DOMAIN

Higher Education Context (General)

Driving Forces

- The focus is on learning.
- There are current examples of effective use of action learning in academe.
- Learners desire relevancy of learning to real life.

Restraining Forces

- The emphasis is on formal learning and curriculum.
- Professors are reluctant to pass more control to learners

Most action learning programs in higher education are found in schools of education at university level and usually aimed at adult education and HRD; that will be addressed shortly. To a lesser degree, schools of business have begun to use action learning programs. One noteworthy example is at Rice University in Houston, Texas. An advertisement for its business school in 2001 says:

> We Educate Business Leaders—leaders for the new companies, the new products. We surveyed CEOs about what they find lacking in the MBA grads they hire. They said leadership and communication skills. We listened. Our action learning curriculum is the result. We're one of two business schools that requires every student to work with real businesses as part of their education.

Action learning has made no major inroads in higher education (in general) beyond this example and the examples we will provide below from adult education and HRD. As indicated earlier in the book, we view higher education as the most difficult context to work with from an action learning standpoint. The formal curriculum orientation can be extremely difficult to overcome.

One potential inroad for those seeking a way to gain a toehold for action learning in academe is through service learning initiatives linked to the community. Such programs most easily take root in schools of education and social work where the service orientation is high. Action learning can provide an ideal modality in this type of application, yet we know of only one program that seems to fit this mold. It is a part of the Educational Leadership Program at Florida Atlantic University. Begun in 2000, this action learning program involves working with problems in the local public school systems. Several action learning sets operated in 2000–2001, and in almost every case the recommendations arrived at moved to the implementation stage.

When starting a program in higher education, you really need someone within the faculty who has the understanding and clout to get a pilot program in place.

Adult Education and HRD

Driving Forces	Restraining Forces
• There is a receptivity to the andragogical model. • There is a willingness to vary learning approaches to include the experiential. • Adult educators profess to be learner centered, interested in having adults determine for themselves what is relevant and what is not relevant.	• Adult educators can practice theory-in-use (formal learning) to relative exclusion of informal learning, even while espousing andragogy. • Adult educators can be a very small enclave, embedded in someone else's curriculum, with limited leverage regarding curriculum redesign (e.g., adult ed and HRD faculty surrounded by K-12 educators).

The major inroads in higher education have been through adult education and HRD programs. Noteworthy examples are Virginia Commonwealth University, George Washington University, Georgia State University, George Mason University, Eastern Connecticut State University, and until 2001, when the program was discontinued, the University of Texas at Austin.

The most notable existing program in action learning and probably the largest is the Revans Institute for Action Learning and Research at the University of Salford in England. The Business School at the University of Ballarat in Australia has an action learning program in its master's of business management degree. The program at the University of Texas was apparently undone by interest in returning to a more traditional curriculum approach, even though it appears that the program had "earned its spurs" and was highly successful.

In the case of universities, they divide up this way in terms of joint problems orientation versus Everyone Bring Your Own (EBO) problem structure:

Joint
- Virginia Commonwealth University
- Georgia State University

EBO
- George Washington University
- University of Texas
- University of Salford
- University of Ballarat
- Revans Institute for Action Learning and Research

When you focus in on the Virginia Commonwealth University, George Washington University, Georgia State University, University of Texas, and the Revans Institute programs, they share at least seven common things:

1. Real world problems/projects.

2. Project focus outside the university.

3. Some personal risk-taking involved.

4. Work on extremely difficult problems/projects either encouraged or predetermined.

5. Students operating in action learning sets.

6. Extensive exposure (e.g., full semester).

7. Some form of set facilitation.

Action Learning in Various Domains, Contexts, and Cultures 131

Pluses and minuses that can be associated with university-based programs in adult education and HRD are as follows:

Pluses

- Students take on tough challenges in a supportive and collaborative environment.
- The program can build self-efficacy and belief in the ability to overcome difficult challenges.
- Real-world problem provides hands-on opportunities for application of knowledge.
- The program builds leadership and problem-solving abilities while strengthening learning to learn capabilities.
- The level of student engagement tends to far surpass traditional classroom experience.

Minuses

- The program tends to be countercultural in academic settings (challenges traditional methods and status quo).
- Risks assumed can create stress, cause anxieties, and trigger intra-group/set conflict because of intensity.
- Not all students (or faculty) are comfortable with relative independence and prefer being told and held to a highly structured format.

The programs at Virginia Commonwealth University and Georgia State University (institutions we are with) follow Revans's philosophy and share the following characteristics:

1. Problem is real, is addressed in real time, and is highly complex.
2. Learners operate in joint project areas that are usually totally unfamiliar to them (by design).
3. A solution set for the problem is expected, but learning is paramount, a balance being struck between action and reflection.
4. Emphasis is on questioning insight (the Q factor).

5. Action learning is to lead to action.

6. Set has no assigned leader.

7. Facilitator jump-starts process, while minimizing interference with the learning being generated within the set itself.

One of the consistent yields from university-based adult education and HRD specific programs in action learning is that they work in two ways. First, they invariably provide the client with something of high value that extends well beyond the solution options otherwise considered. There are usually a multitude of "ah ha's." Secondly, the students frequently indicate that the challenge exceeded any other academic program they had experienced *and* that the learning far surpassed a normal course experience.

The student evaluations of an action learning experience can obviously be of help in bolstering program acceptance. However, the kind of opposition that can spring up when introducing action learning to a curriculum does not necessarily play out of logic. Action learning simply looks different, defies the long-engrained principle of the professor in absolute control of the learners and what occurs in the classroom. The latter is learning by formula (for example, students have twelve set frameworks, units, or modules they must master to successfully complete the course) versus not knowing the outcome, or what will necessarily occur along the way in the learning experience. There can also be risk aversion—what if the project for the client fails and the school dean hears about it? You have to trust the process.

How can you beat the odds in introducing action learning in an adult education and HRD curriculum, or for that matter, in higher education, in general?

1. Understand the nature of action learning in contrast to other programs.

2. Gain an advocate or advocates.

3. Use the professors at other universities who have successful

action learning programs to help inform and convince your academic colleagues.

4. Do a pilot program first. It may take a couple of years to shake it down so that it fits cleanly in your culture and circumstances. Action learning, like set composition, is more art than science.

5. Do not be nervous and move to intervene the first time there is a kink in the hose. Sometimes you do need to move decisively, but more often than not, you need to stand back, avoid meddling, and allow the process to unfold. To repeat something we hold dear, *trust the process*. If the process is set up correctly, it will work, and the learners themselves will work hard to make certain it occurs. They are usually at least as fully vested as you are.

Why do you want to expend the effort to get an action learning program up and running in an adult education and HRD program? First, action learning represents a full expression of adult learning. It is andragogy being practiced. Because of the high energy and motivation levels it can generate in the learners, it can be extraordinarily fulfilling for the professor as well as the students.

Community Colleges

Driving Forces	Restraining Forces
• There is a willingness to experiment and move with the times.	• There is a predominance of formal curricula.
• Students seek relevancy and ways to deal with real problems and obstacles to career growth.	• The high density of adjunct faculty can work against action learning approaches (e.g., lack of identity with the institution).

Some of us view the community college movement as a primary engine of change and key promoter of life-long learning.

Jobs are now changing rapidly, with entire occupational categories either disappearing or undergoing major reframing. Retraining of workers and upgrading of skills become continuous. This all centers on relevancy of the learning; and community colleges can be better at ensuring this than four-year traditional universities. The real-world, real-time problems associated with action learning are clearly a good match with the mission of community colleges. In fact, they can be engaging in a form of action learning in some cases without recognizing the linkage. One example is in the auto maintenance area, where teams of students can jointly troubleshoot and diagnose complex problems. Working with the electronics of a car today requires a tremendous level of skill and insight.

We feel that action learning programs can and should be used in the community college setting, and for reasons that go beyond development of occupational skill sets. Many of the adults who enroll in community college programs feel significant risk. Their self-confidence levels can be at low ebb following a corporate downsizing. They are undergoing both a career transition in many cases as well as a life transition. Some entering students will have been out of high school for a period of time or in the process of completing their GED through high school or community college based programs. The first school experience may have left lingering bad memories. This is a well-documented phenomenon. Action learning, because it involves the opportunity to conquer difficult challenges in a supportive environment (including other students in a similar transition), can bolster the spirit and elevate self-efficacy. This can be as important in gaining meaningful employment as skill sets that are occupationally specific.

The banding together of faculty to engage in action learning projects can be productive. For example, it is easy to see the value of having a group of faculty members work together to sort through the environmental pressures of the economy and marketplace in relation to curriculum. What works against this is the number of adjunct faculty members employed. They can be the overwhelming majority of the faculty. What incentive do they have to address problems of the institution? Their focus can

Action Learning in Various Domains, Contexts, and Cultures 135

be largely confined to the courses they teach. Further, their primary employment is probably elsewhere. This is an obvious constraint.

We feel that the same fundamental approaches used in adult education and HRD programs at university level can work in community colleges with the aforementioned caveats.

Adult Education Outside Academe
(Examples are adult basic education and English-as-a second language programs)

Driving Forces	Restraining Forces
• Adult students have real needs such as literacy and basic skills, and want learning to immediately deal with real-world essentials.	• Many of the teachers (upwards of 90 percent) come from a K–12 background, and operate out of a pedagogical framework. • Programs can be adult education in name only. • These are bare bones programs in terms of financing and deal with a clientele that can be considered down and out and lacking in political influence. • There is usually little incentive or impetus to change.

While on the surface, this can seem an unproductive arena to enter, Dilworth has done extensive research in the area of adult literacy and basic skills. There are, in fact, a number of ways that action learning could be employed in the adult basic education (ABE) area. One of the best concepts encountered was put forward by Karl Haigler of the Salem Company in the early 1990s. Haigler's thought was that you teach ABE by engaging students in the jury trial process, such as reading the transcripts (even attending trials), writing an interpretation, and sharing their views. In Haigler's view, you would realize the corollary benefit of having the participants learn more about how democracy works. It becomes a citizenship education program, as well as one targeted at building the adult literacy level and basic skills. Action learning could also be applied to reading of manuals and documentation directly related to the occupational area or workplace, with the learners/action learning set determining how the material can be improved. Some ABE programs in companies do involve having the learners read everyday material, rather than review workbooks having nothing to do with the work environment.

For the reasons shown in the Force Field Analysis, employment of action learning in this context will tend to be a nonstarter, but that should not dissuade us from striving to make inroads.

BUSINESS/SERVICE RELATED DOMAIN

Major Private Companies

Driving Forces

- Management may welcome learning approaches that can bolster competitive advantage.
- The use of action learning in business is growing.
- Action learning fits well with development of self-directed work teams.

Restraining Forces

- There are hierarchical power structures.
- Some companies have a fixation with formal learning methodologies.
- Traditional HRD practitioners can be one of the major inhibitors because of classroom focus.

As outlined earlier in the book, and in considerable detail, GE stands out in its long-standing use of action learning. The company has also been uniquely successful.

There is a long and growing list of companies using action

learning. Applications come in a wide range of configurations. We provide several examples, fairly representative, but without revealing the company since there are confidentiality agreements in place.

Example 1

This large company decided to offer an industry-specific MBA program to employees. The company entered a relationship with a university in order to do this. The front-end of the program was simulation based. Action learning sets of four to five members were formed. Their initial challenge was to work on time-driven requirements in a realistic and highly complex simulation. This created a bonding effect and led to team forming and norming. Facilitator consultants schooled in action learning entered as the simulation was drawing to a close. The sets were then given a real problem of great significance to the company to work on. The learning coaches worked with the sets in outlining action learning principles, such as the need to balance action and reflection.

Example 2

Client problems were developed and assigned to groups of six to eight within the company. The learning coaches helped the sets norm, coached them through action learning principles, and served as a resource to them as they worked toward problem resolutions over a period of several months.

Example 3

Teams/sets were formed, and taken to a facility in a different U.S. state to discuss how the company could become more global. They developed their views over a period of days (one thinks of the change acceleration program at GE). They were then flown to China for two weeks to walk the ground and see how their conclusions really worked in a real live global environment. They then came home and compared notes—what they thought about strategies for globalizing the company before the site visit in China, as compared with their views after the country visit.

Summary

There can be a tendency within companies to set up what are really task forces and call it action learning, as if the only thing necessary for action learning is a real problem with people to work on it. We reiterate: by definition, the learning in action learning is equal to or in many cases takes priority over task performance. A problem solved or a task performed has limited value if in the process there is no gain in learning or capacity to learn. There is a growing receptivity to action learning in large companies as a result of reported successes elsewhere. GE is frequently a reference point.

Corporate Universities

Driving Forces

- Meister model (described in this section) recognizes importance of action learning.
- Companies like GE can practice action learning and use their corporate university to seed it.

Restraining Forces

- Corporate university can be a limited makeover of old training department, with its rigidities and preferences for classroom instruction.

The basic reference point for corporate universities today is arguably Jeanne Meister's book, *Corporate Universities* (1998). Her model is the one that seems to serve as the start point in setting up such a university. The number of such institutions has been exploding.

> As of 1997 the number of working adults participating in some form of training program at 100 corporate universities equaled the student enrollment at 125 universities of Michigan, assuming a 1996 total enrollment of 36,500. (p. 12)

In other words, the number of working adults at the 100 corporate universities Meister alluded to equals 125 times a University of Michigan enrollment of 36,500 or 4.5 million participants.

Meister clearly believes that action learning is an important ingredient in corporate universities.

> Rather than simply sending high potential managers to external executive education programs, these organizations are developing focused, large-scale customized action learning programs with measurable results. These hands-on, application-driven programs are based on actual business challenges facing an organization and give participants an opportunity to actively discuss, diagnose and recommend solutions to real-life business challenges. (p. 15)

Corporate universities can be as much a mosaic of resources as an institution standing separately. They can be tightly interwoven with community colleges and other universities. They can even be virtual (Dell Computer), existing only in cyberspace, with all learning opportunities dealt with interactively on line. They can also be sizable institutions, even offering courses to other corporations on a reimbursable basis, making the corporate university a profit center. On the other hand, all courses being offered can be essentially restricted to employees internal to the organization. Sprint University, in Kansas City, has over 400 faculty, limits its courses to its own employees and has a capital budget akin to many private universities.

Corporate universities can be fertile ground for action learning. They can also inhibit action learning because of their focus on formal training products and curricula. Some of the same basic points made in relation to adult education and HRD programs apply here. The corporate university has both some of the vested interests of a regular university and those of a corporate HRD department. On balance, the scales seem to tip toward the corporate HRD orientation. The type of courses offered generally fit better with the curricula of a community college than with a university.

Corporate universities come in all sizes and shapes. They can be a small shoehorn operation or rather vast in their scope, such as GE Crotonville or Motorola University. Since the cultures and specific settings within this context can vary widely, careful advance scoping is a must.

New Economy Businesses

Driving Forces

- You cannot ignore this context. It is growing and will continue to grow.
- The need to move swiftly and deal with real problems is intensified.

Restraining Forces

- Operating virtually limits or obviates face-to-face contact and complicates action learning set formation and dynamics.

There are companies that hire, train, and terminate employees without ever having had them inside the physical plant of the company. No one within the company may ever meet them between hire and termination. Gary May, the first chief learning officer (CLO) in the country, once indicated that this was often the case in his company, Millbrook Distribution Services. For companies whose product is an on-line service, market research and sales training take on very different aspects. Training customers across the globe in the procedures for using online services may take priority over in-house training, limiting employee development opportunities at home base. These are different paradigms of adult education and HRD than we are accustomed to dealing with.

It is not uncommon for a team to be formed to operate virtually. Team members may never meet in person. The team can be global with individuals from different countries comprising the team. Little has been written about what this means in terms of group dynamics. Colky, Colky, and Young (2002) have addressed managing and developing people in the virtual organization. We consider this a valuable reference in understanding this emerging phenomenon.

The new economy is coming to the academic setting as well, and sometimes it can raise serious questions. Few would disagree with the premise that human resource development professionals need to understand how to deal with others interpersonally (which can include serving as a learning coach or facilitator), yet, as noted in Chapter 2, there is at least one master's program in HRD being offered by a major university entirely on line. Further, student teams of roughly six are formed, brought together only on the basis of compatibility of time zone. There are no efforts made to guide team building, even though the students are expected to operate as a team.

We believe that action learning can work well in new economy businesses, because it focuses on acceleration of the learning process, a focus shared by such businesses. We also believe that action learning can work virtually. However, there is a case for having the participants meet and have a chance to bond before reverting to virtual communications, whether teleconference, e-mail, or special network. In any case, thought should be given to who the participants will be. They should also have knowledge of each other's background. In 2002, we did an international action learning project in the United Kingdom and Romania that was conducted virtually for the most part. Both of us had participants prepare written life histories to build understanding.

New software is emerging, specifically Groove, which will allow a group interacting virtually to customize the communications protocols in order to facilitate asynchronous networking.

This area needs much more research. It seems well suited for action learning, but will obviously require some prototyping in determining the best approaches.

Small Businesses and Nonprofits

Driving Forces

- Action learning can provide low cost, effective route to competitiveness.

Restraining Forces

- There is usually a limited financial base.
- Expertise in action learn-

- People are already accustomed to working in small teams to solve problems.

ing within organization is limited or nonexistent.

Small businesses can be an ideal environment in which to practice action learning. They rarely have sufficient funds to conduct formal training programs, and often will have only one or two human resource professionals, who usually dedicate most of their effort to compensation systems. Small businesses, by their very nature, usually operate in small teams so they are already conditioned to that form of operation.

Dilworth was involved with a company of about 150 employees in 2001 as they were about to set up a new assembly line. An action learning set of graduate students was brought in to work with the CEO and his staff in hiring the new people, training them, and developing an incentive program. This was a nice case of synergy. The student effort came at no cost to the company, the students ended up with an outstanding learning experience, and the company ended up learning how to employ action learning in other areas. We believe that this type of action learning partnership should be given priority by universities. It provides a needed service to the company, and because you are working with a small client, there can usually be more direct and immediate interaction between client and external action learning set. Communication lines are short.

GOVERNMENT ORGANIZATIONS

Federal

Driving Forces

- There is the drive to improve performance (e.g., National Performance Review).

Restraining Forces

- Legislative constraints and regulatory guidance and standards are a reality.

Action Learning in Various Domains, Contexts, and Cultures   143

- There is a growing emphasis on learning from approaches successful in private business.

- Program design can be wedded to classroom instruction.

The federal government has not been a major user of action learning, at least under that label. One program, launched in 1999 by the Federal Executive Institute in Charlottesville, Virginia, involved use of action learning with Senior Executive Service employees scheduled for training at the institute.

There are probably a number of reasons why action learning programs are not more common in the federal government. One reason is the deeply embedded predilection for formal learning approaches. However, when you look beyond formal labeling of things as being action learning programs, there are, in fact, some powerful programs in existence. One of the best such programs centers on the National Training Center of the U.S. Army at Fort Irwin, California. Here Army combat units, including subteams (e.g., squads) spend a full week in the desert maneuvering against opposing forces (OPFOR) in around-the-clock, combat-like conditions. At the end of the exercise there is a detailed after-action review with unit members engaged in deep discourse and reflection. Revans would probably rule this out as genuine action learning on the basis of it being a simulation of reality. However, we feel it clearly qualifies as action learning. There is no prefabricated script. Both the participating unit and OPFOR respond spontaneously to events, creating the scenario that eventually unfolds. After the Gulf War in 1991, U.S. Army soldiers would commonly say: "This was a lot easier than the National Training Center. That was really a war!"

Some of the executive development programs within the armed forces also qualify as action learning. The programs at the Senior Service Colleges in Department of Defense can involve dealing with real-world issues in arriving at recommendations. It can also involve sending the students to other countries to examine issues first-hand, with dialogue and reflection occurring throughout the experience. Beyond Department of Defense, there is only a smattering of action learning within the federal government. Because government increasingly strives to model itself after successful programs in industry, action learning can be expected to gradually establish a presence in the federal government.

State

Driving Forces

- Lack of funds for training programs can encourage alternative methods, for example, action learning.
- Some states are becoming incubators for best practices.

Restraining Forces

- The environment can be extremely rigid and bureaucratic.
- The system can lack an HRD capability sufficient to deal with methods beyond the classroom.
- The orientation is to classroom instruction.

States, to our best knowledge, are not heavy users of action learning. State governments vary widely. Some are inspired in terms of using advanced methods. Other states are far behind the times, with little likelihood of getting better any time soon. State systems can be extremely bureaucratic. The urge to justify all expenditures—and the thirst by legislatures for proof of money well spent—operates against the introduction of action learning. Action learning can almost sound like psychobabble to those whose assumptions about learning and accountability lead them to demand evidence of instant results.

While what occurs at state level can be quite uneven, there are cases of programs that seem to be very close to action learning in concept and principle. The Virginia Department of Transportation has an exemplary mentorship program where students can be paired with a mentor as part of a co-op program. It allows the student to grapple with real-world issues and then reflect on the issue and how to solve it in concert with the mentor (in effect a learning coach).

The problems at state level that inhibit growing support for action learning programs are multifaceted—bureaucracy, funding support, mental set, and frequently lack of a highly skilled HRD staff to accomplish basic HRD things, let alone action learning.

County/Municipal

Driving Forces

- Innovative environments exist at the local level (Osborne's laboratories of democracy).
- People are already accustomed to working in small teams to solve problems.

Restraining Forces

- There is a limited financial base.
- There is a lack of well-developed HRD capability.
- Programs can be bound by local and state rules that restrict flexibility.

There can be strong surfacing of innovative thought at the local level. A prime example is the City of Hampton, Virginia. In 1995, it was the overall excellence winner of the Optima Award, presented annually by the *Personnel Journal*, finishing ahead of Pepsico, 3M, and others, as the only non–private sector firm in the running. The city government has employed approaches to employee empowerment that fall in the area of action learning, among them the mixing of staff in cross-functional groups in addressing problems of major significance to the city.

Henrico County, Virginia, earned a prestigious award from the American Society for Training and Development in 1998 for the excellence of its programs, albeit not in the action learning area. However, its organization and HR capability seem sufficient to introduce action learning programs.

When you go to the county and municipal level, you obviously are at another order of magnitude when it comes to the number of variations in organizational culture and capability you can encounter. It can almost seem infinite. The best formula for introducing action learning to counties and municipalities is along the lines discussed for small businesses. You look for synergy, as in the case of the Virginia Commonwealth and Georgia State University graduate student teams that introduce action learning to the organizations with whom they partner. To the extent you have organizational role models, like the City of Hampton, they can help leverage innovative initiatives in other municipalities.

WORLD

International Organizations
(Examples are United Nations, World Bank, World Health Organization)

Driving Forces

- Much of the world is inclined to relationship building, as opposed to the more time-driven impersonal style of U.S. and European cultures.

Restraining Forces

- Systems can be bureaucratically rigid.
- Operating cross-culturally can produce constraints.
- Program planners will tend to have a didactic classroom approach in mind.

When dealing with international organizations, you inherently have to operate cross-culturally, meaning that action learning approaches will need to be acculturated. Because of the mix of cultures, the dynamics can be difficult to decipher. Asian cultures, for example, will tend to hold back expression of true feelings. That can leave you guessing. If you are operating with European cultures, you need to understand that not all cultures are necessarily similar. The British and German cultures, like that in the United States, tend to be monochronic—time driven and linear, one step at a time. The French are polychronic—able to deal with several things simultaneously and not necessarily in sequential order. Other European cultures may lie somewhere in between.

Action Learning in Various Domains, Contexts, and Cultures   147

Because culture can be so complex, it is best to partner with someone who both understands the predominant culture (for example, Chinese) and your culture. There are no set rules for employing action learning cross-culturally, but the following need to be kept in mind in forming action learning sets that are cross-national/cultural:

1. Some cultures are extremely status conscious (including seniority in terms of age). It is wise to ensure that participants are at the same status and age level (this can be significant in dealing with Asian cultures).

2. Some cultures (for example, Middle Eastern) do not necessarily accept having men and women in the same team or set. Nevertheless, in international organizations, the protocol will tend to prescribe gender equality. Traditions of the home culture can be parked at the door when operating in the international realm, but even if that is the case, you need to be sensitive to potential underlying dynamics.

3. Many cultures operate on the basis of formal instruction with the instructor as authority figure. The egalitarianism of an action learning set may be foreign to them. There may be a need for some pre-orientation and pre-work in setting the stage for action learning.

Nongovernment Organizations (NGOs)
(Examples are Doctors Without Borders, International Red Cross)

Driving Forces

- NGOs can be inclined to accept action learning as a natural learning modality because of its comfortable fit with relationship-oriented cultures (Hofstede's collectivism versus individualism).

Restraining Forces

- Many of the same rigidities associated with international organizations in general can be found in NGOs.
- NGOs tend to have strong tilt toward classroom instruction.

On balance, NGOs are probably easier to work with than those organizations that tend to be more formalized structures, such as those in the United Nations. NGOs tend to have an entrepreneurial, situationally planned, business case way of operating. They can be more receptive to approaches like action learning that promise to build their capabilities and enhance their versatility. The cautions about cross-cultural sensitivities expressed for other international bodies apply here as well.

SYSTEM CHANGERS

Organization Development (OD)

Driving Forces

- Action learning aligns closely with organization development and is even considered a preferred intervention in remolding corporate culture.
- Practitioners have the skill sets necessary to introduce and sustain action learning programs.

Restraining Forces

- Organization development, like action learning, can elicit major resistances because of its perceived threat to existing power relationships.
- Cultures not ready to receive major change.
- Expert focus of organization development practitioners can run counter to action learning.

As indicated, action learning has a natural place in the repertoire of organization development. At GE, action learning (and specifically the work-out approach) is expressly viewed as an organization development intervention strategy. Many of the steps associated with organization development, including gaining an understanding of the organizational culture, can also be tied to action learning. Once organization development professionals are schooled in action learning, they can become prime agents in introducing action learning in an organization and possibly even blending it with other organization development strategies. Both initiatives aim at organizational change, with the thought of increasing organizational capacity. If creation of learning organizations, capable of rapid adaptation, is an important goal, then action learning represents a good complementary fit with other organization development models in bringing this about.

Chief Learning Officer (CLO)

Driving Forces	Restraining Forces
• Based on the very nature of their role, CLOs are inclined to experiment with alternative learning approaches.	• Even CLOs sitting at the right hand of the CEO can have a struggle getting HRD practitioners to break out of a classroom-driven mindset.
• CLOs have position power to mount and support learning initiatives.	• The novelty of this position makes much that CLOs do seem "out of character" to others in the organization.

Because CLOs are relatively new in the corporate structure, there is still a sort-out going on concerning how to engineer the CLO role. Willis invented the concept and titling of the CLO and has watched both the idea and confusion about it spread rapidly across the corporate landscape. The CLO is intended to be the executive who envisions and instigates the processes necessary to create an organization that learns continuously, realizing that "learning how to learn" is the primary target.

A certain mysticism pervades notions of what a learning organization looks like, beyond recognizing that the rate of learning and adaptation capabilities improve markedly. Consequently, CLOs do not yet have the same portfolios or have the same level of influence in every organization. To further complicate matters, there can be chief knowledge officers (CKOs) whose work is also related to learning processes. Still others have the title of chief training officer (CTO). Willis believes the variations in titles and roles are related to contextual assumptions about what learning is and how it is best accomplished. The four common assumptions explored in Chapter 2 are a case in point.

Not uncommonly, a CLO will have some organization development background. Certainly, there is compatibility between what a CLO at executive level is trying to achieve and what action learning has to offer. It can be a natural, though not necessarily obvious, marriage.

Other HRD Practitioners

Driving Forces

- Leading-edge HRD academic programs are broadening the reach of what constitutes effective learning delivery, to include action learning.

Restraining Forces

- Even when HRD is operative in a company, it is usually dominated by human resource (HR) systems that are more involved with compensation, recruitment, and employee assistance than learning.
- Anything outside traditional programs can be viewed as "soft" or as a threat.

HR can, by its tendency to concentrate on what can be called human resource management functions, squeeze out the ability to deal with learning. When there is a training function internal to HR, it will usually be dedicated to delivery of course packages, some of which may be prescribed by government regulations. There may be few, if any, HRD professionals on the staff. When Dilworth was in charge of HR for a state agency with 6,000 employees, he was initially given two trainers and they had very little capability beyond rather straightforward platform instruction skills.

To introduce action learning in organizations can require

Action Learning in Various Domains, Contexts, and Cultures 151

the direct advocacy of a CLO or other highly placed advocate. If the organization does not have advanced HRD capabilities in-house, it will probably be necessary to bring in outsiders to assist. The assistance can include both organizing the action learning program and then helping to build a cadre of people who can engineer action learning initiatives within the organization. They do not have to be situated in the HR function (especially if, as is increasingly the case, HRD exists as a separate unit and sponsors the learning efforts), but it is wise to build capability and understanding of the action learning process within HR whenever possible.

SUMMARY

There are many contexts within which action learning can be employed. As already emphasized, you need to understand the context. Each context has special characteristics associated with it that will require customization of the action learning programs. Assumptions deeply ingrained in organizations about what learning is and how it happens must be taken into account. International programs can present special challenges.

CHAPTER 7

The Transformative Potential of Action Learning

What appears to be important is to be in at the birth of a new insight, not necessarily one's own, when there bursts forth that gasp of surprise which reveals that, at last, somebody has suddenly seen a new relationship that brings new perspectives to his world.
—Reginald W. Revans (1982, p. 603)

By far the most significant learning experience in adulthood involves critical self-reflection—reassessing our own orientation to perceiving, knowing, believing, feeling, and acting . . . Reflection on one's own premises can lead to transformative learning [authors' emphasis].
—Jack Mezirow & Associates (1990, p. 13)

Action learning combines individual responsibility and reflection on personal experience with comprehensive attention to the multiple perspectives of various stakeholders within a social unit . . .
—Victoria Marsick (in Mezirow & Associates, 1990, p. 43)

We confess that we began this chapter as most researchers do, dipping into our extensive, indexed database for the evidence of personal transformations that the participants themselves say they have experienced in action learning. We knew we would easily find these because one of our prime index terms is *transformation*. Then we came to a sudden (and of course reflective) pause.

We have made much of the fact that, although applications of action learning are worldwide, they are also distinguished by context. Therefore, we need to discuss transformative experiences in the contexts of a changing world, changing organizations, and changing human lives.

We really have no choice but to put action learning in larger societal contexts if we are to keep pace with Revans's own visionary, profoundly inclusive way of thinking and operating. What seems to delight him most, even now, is knowledge that action learning is spreading everywhere. The hundreds of contacts—at all ranks from villagers to kings—that he has made throughout the world are not only constantly renewed in correspondence with him, but are also consistently serving to help make action learning an instrument for deeper human understanding.

THE WORLD CHANGES BEFORE OUR VERY EYES

The tragedy that came to U.S. shores on the morning of September 11, 2001, revealed to everyone in the world within reach of mass communications that instant, ideological mass annihilation of civilians is not only possible, but actually happened. Incredibly, it was even welcomed in some contexts. But *there is also a worldwide sense of the depth of the tragedy, and the need for transformative thinking, processes, and actions has never seemed more acute.*

Across the globe, we have traded condolences as if we were indeed one family. New and previously unthinkable personal, national, and organizational alliances —at varying depth and understandably hemmed in by cautious reservations—have been forged. Unprecedented actions on a global scale have been taken with far-reaching consequences.

In *Common Fire,* Daloz and others suggest that the American idea of democracy demands a "commons," a public space that marks "the center of the shared world" where people can, despite sharp differences, meet, converse, and work out what actions may be for the common good (1996, pp. 2–3). It occurs to us that this notion of the village commons, expanded into the realm of global conversations, may explain why so many people from so many nations were at work in the World Trade Center. It may also go far toward explaining why the terrible loss of this new kind of commons—a bustling, bartering center in an urbanized society—together with all the well-intentioned, hardworking, ordinary people it contained or touched, is inconsolable.

Handy (1996) has said that

> ... people have to draw back from life occasionally, to concentrate on the things that really matter. When people are very busy they lose themselves in their busy-ness and are unaware of anything apart from the little bit of the world that they are occupying. (p. 45)

The danger that he sees in this is that "life, our life, is changing beyond all recognition. All certainty has gone, leaving behind unanswered questions and a new freedom." He spoke long before the tragedy, and certainly he is not the only voice telling us that, although old answers won't do, when we leave these old answers behind we are free to learn. In fact, we cannot do otherwise.

When everyone can know as much as the next person, he believes, we still have the residual wisdom inside of each of us—our tacit knowing—that can be tapped to inform our actions both individually and collectively. This rich, internal residual is precisely what action learning brings so powerfully to expression. And it is precisely why we have emphasized the value of set variety as well as "strangeness" or unfamiliarity in the situations and contexts action learners are asked to address. It is also the basis for demanding that action learners work on real problems. To step back to case studies or simulations or canned curriculum allows the learners to "live in their heads" and confront problems on an intellectual, rather than a consequential level.

Transformations of society, self, world, all seem to require triggering events. That is, it is the things we have experienced that serve as catalysts and make it appear necessary for us to act in ways we have not acted before, thinking new thoughts that we have not thought before.

THE THINGS THAT JUST DON'T FIT

It does not matter what we call the events, the information, the processes we encounter in our lives that just don't fit our understandings and expectations. Whether we say anomaly, dissonance, or catastrophe, we are all aware that what we experience often *is* incredible and goes unexplained. We have sought scientific certainty, and what we have found instead is a new science of uncertainties.

Hawkins cites the work of Briggs and Peat (*Turbulent Mirrors*) in the following quote within a quote:

> ... chaos theory provides the basis for a cosmopolitan human commonality based on a common humility and mutual dependency stemming from our universal ignorance concerning what is going to happen next; or how on earth to control it when it does. It reveals "a universe that is vaster, more complex, more fluid, less secure, and in a sense more frightening than the one that has been portrayed ... " But it is also conducive to comradeship, to fellowship, "because we are all in it together." (Hawkins, 1995, p. 40)

The interesting thing about this quotation is that it is a very good description of action learning, when the "universe" is interpreted to mean the context, the problem, the set that is acting in and on it, and the people in the set that are mutually interacting. Thus, the quotation makes connections for us between the new world we have not yet come to embrace, the new social imperatives for community and caring, the new uncertainty science that sometimes seems so counterintuitive, and the new commons (if we may call it that) that is a worthy metaphor for action learning. Sets tend to develop a village square sort of intimacy, with honest conversations that lead to action for the common good. A participant's reflection from a recent set exemplifies this:

> The group, for me, provided the greatest amount of learning. Never before had I been able to trust that "what needed doing would get done," in a group function. I was amazed at the selflessness and camaraderie that was exhibited. Many times individual members would adjust their schedules to take on additional tasks in order that the team could be more effective. This was a wonderful learning experience.

SYSTEM GAMMA AS GROWTH MEDIUM OF ACTION LEARNING

In earlier chapters, we have concentrated mainly on what action learning is, what Revans says about it, what our own experience with it has been, and what needs to be paid attention to in contexts where it is introduced. But we have also run sneak previews of action learning outcomes in nearly every chapter, because these outcomes are so striking and provide such graphic illustrations of the power in egalitarian, leaderless learning with and from each other. We have seen extraordinary change—both incremental and transformational—in individuals and organizations because of action learning.

Collecting and analyzing text units from action learners' reflective essays over a number of years, we find consistent positive effects across contexts and geographic locations. While negative incidents are faithfully recorded when they occur, action learners place enormous value on what they have learned from these setbacks as well as from the affirmations they have received in the course of struggling with the work and trading their insights. What participants in the United States have expressed tallies well with what is found in similar texts examined in the United Kingdom, Australia, and Africa: Action learning not only makes people different, it makes the situations they address and act upon far different, too. To quote Revans, "self-knowledge is gold in the mind," becoming the coin of both organizational change and individual growth and transformation (Revans, 1982, p. 766).

The evidence, that System Gamma (the changing self in the midst of the changing situation) thrives in what Revans calls symbiotic relationship with the Alpha definitional and Beta discovery systems, is very strong. All three systems feed off each other and wither if any of the three is missing or incomplete. Their mutuality is critical. If the problem is hastily and inadequately chosen, "peeled," and redefined, the process breaks down. If participants think they already have the answers and do not take the need for going through the bartering of questions, assumptions, and ideas seriously as they take action, the process breaks down. If there is little to no interest in learning about the self in relation to the work at hand and the people at hand, the process falls apart in like measure. Our data shows this beyond the shadow of a doubt.

On the other hand, individuals in their respective sets take heart when there is any kind of breakthrough in any of the systems. When they have produced something of worth, either in product form or in deeper understanding, the whole set feels rewarded. Those who are not fully invested at the beginning tend to become so, not only because they are driven by urgency of the need to perform, but also because the quest for new insight is contagious.

While Systems Alpha and Beta carry the weight of the problem investigation, it is Gamma that carries the insights. It explicitly requires the action learner to investigate the problem in relation to self, and to examine both self and problem in relation to others. It is naturally open to multiple influences of environments both internal and external as well as personal and organizational. It does not require call-up of reflection time by the administrative intervention of a learning coach. Our experience tells us that all that is needed is the recognition, by everyone connected with the set, that System Gamma is always present in individuals who are interacting, especially when that interaction is "up-front and personal" in small groups.

Gamma is just "there" as part of the process. As the scope of (and attention to) the real problem expands, so too, the inquiry deepens. People are more deeply affected, they see the value of taking time to do what they are doing, and so the opportunity for organizational impact widens.

PARTICIPANTS SPEAK FOR THEMSELVES

The participants themselves do not mince words. While the gains they specify range in intensity from simple learning through questioning how to make better decisions, to complex learning about how to reinvent themselves and their thinking, they are aware that something important has happened to them. Many realize quickly that the impact of action learning is not over when the program ends, and the wish is often expressed that learning of this sort would never end. For those who have just been through some of the most grueling hours they have ever experienced, gratitude for the struggle and wishing for it to continue are notable endorsements of action learning.

One of the post-event questions Willis asks action learners to reflect upon is, "What is different now?" There is seldom any doubt that changes have occurred, although learners cannot always immediately specify the nature of the changes. As one action learning essayist said, ".... I am changed by this experience although at this point, I am not quite able to say how."

Here in their own words are a sampling of statements and narratives of what stood out for participants in the course of their action learning. Some of the comments are provided by the clients, not the outside set members, in cases where these clients have been either closely associated with set activity or have actually participated as part of the set in the hybrid, single problem, joint project model of action learning discussed in Chapter 4.

While the stories and new understandings expressed by the essayists can easily stand on their own, we have chosen to weave them into the fabric of this book alternately with our own reflections and the reflections of Mezirow and Revans, mentors to whom we are particularly indebted for their useful framing of ideas about learning that transforms consciousness. We also offer useful reflections of other writers, wanting not to convey the impression that wisdom about learning how to learn is confined to a select few. The essay writers remain anonymous because of the intensely personal nature of their comments, although all have given permission for their statements to be used in our ongoing research and writing.

Four Stories to Ponder

Story 1

We begin with an extended story, declaring an irreversible change that occurred for an American woman in an international action learning set meeting across an ocean from her home. The story is a prime example of the heightening effects of total immersion in action learning (process immersion), having to work with others unlike herself (set diversity), and experiencing life for the first time away from her familiar surroundings (far from home). These are the action learning conditions that we have identified as particularly conducive to transformative learning (Willis & Dilworth, 2000).

Her story is a study in critical self-reflection, triggered in the context of a hospital merger problem her set was working on. She had no background in health services and was called upon to think entirely out of the box of her discipline and life experience.

> Through interaction, in a variety of places, I learned, absorbed, reflected on life, learning, group dynamics, styles, and mostly, myself. There was a stripping away process that commenced when the course began. First, I was taken out of my usual physical environment. Then, I was removed from my routines. Later, my surroundings changed (three times). I was away from my family and most of my friends. Phones and televisions were no longer there to fall into, many other distracting comforts were not present . . . The people around me were different, the culture was different, even the food was different. I was left with me, just me. I am not quite sure who I thought I was. I am a lot more

resilient than I thought. Much more adaptable than I gave myself credit for before this trip. So what do I do with these revelations? Do I go back to the same life, job, routines, etc. that I left behind? I cannot. I've thought long and hard about this since I've been back. I cannot come back from the learning on this trip and pretend it didn't happen . . . This essay will probably rewrite itself a hundred times, a hundred different ways.

We do not always know what happens after the reflective essays are turned in. In this particular case, however, we are able to verify that the essayist's learning authentically changed her views of the world, altering her life and career path. We find support here, as in many other essays, for the thesis that wherever possible, the unfamiliar-unfamiliar quadrant needs to be utilized in the design of action learning. It is stripping away of the familiar that breaks open the cocoon of past experience and expectations and amplifies the learning. It is not an exaggeration to apply the term *metamorphosis* to such cases (Barker, 2000, p. 1). The account in Chapter 1 of the parolee who seized upon action learning as a way to break out of his own destructive pattern, his self-incarceration, is another story of this type.

Kennedy (1990) has addressed the "renegotiation" and "metamorphosis" that occur when people encounter points of view that differ from their own. The description seems especially applicable to action learning situations:

> . . . as persons experience other perspectives or sense contradictions within the accepted framework, they often wonder about and question the givens they receive. A helpful metaphor is that of the cocoon . . . Changes occur inside, but the parameters of reality are formed by the limits of the cocoon. In a more complex way, human beings are formed and form themselves within some limited perspective . . . Human beings experience many potential breakthroughs when events in their lives test the perceived parameters or thrust these people "outside," where they can gain some distance from the framework. There, they may question not only the internal contradictions but the limitations themselves. (p. 100)

The individual is required to learn how to learn when the answers to crucial questions lie beyond what Revans calls the "guessable gap" (1982, p. 588). Further, the individual discovers that he or she has *not* been stripped of internal resources, and is perfectly able to turn on the power of self-knowledge in a community of others who are doing the same. Again we quote Revans, relying on his 60 years of experience with the process he named:

> The strength of action learning is that it perpetually forces each participant to examine at depth what he thinks he is doing... In an action learning set each mind is not only exploring itself at a new intensity... but [also] down paths long since overgrown or blocked by the heaps of unsorted experience accumulating year in, year out, through lack of systematic reference (Revans, 1982, p. 730).

The unexamined action and the unexamined life, bound up in each other, are likely the norm, not the exception, and action learning is a way to change the norm not only in the workplace and the schools, but also in the streets. Being swamped with change discourages us from taking time for reflection, but paradoxically, nothing drains the swamp except action we have created through reflection. If in action learning we mirror to each other our shortcomings in understanding and our sincere commitment to solving critical problems, then we are energized to begin anew, with fresh questions and fresh outcomes.

Story 2

This is a shorter story, but it exemplifies the common finding in our data that personal change and organizational change are intimately related. In this case, the writer is a speech and language therapist from the United Kingdom. The action learning model used was the EBO model, and her problem was helping her allied health care organization to expand and institutionalize the use of flextime in providing a wide range of health care, such as physical therapy and foot care. She reported:

> Reflection on the new information generated by my actions... enabled me to repeatedly assess and adjust my internally held models of the organization, my colleagues, and people and change in general... The refusal of action learning to be neatly sepa-

rated into a management development module, its propensity for overflowing out of a given project and into every aspect of work and personal life, demonstrated to me a major difference between learning and training.

She was able to establish new procedures in her own department and also found strong support for similar changes among the chiropodists. While personal and departmental impacts of action learning did not translate into structural or operational changes across the entire organization, they seem to have had an effect on large segments of it and certainly influenced the practices of those with whom she worked most closely (Willis, 2000, p. 512).

Story 3

A university professor who was an action learner in a Francophone country in West Africa explained what happened to him and how he analyzed the set activity (working on a single problem) in this fashion:

> My personal experience with action learning has made me observe that by the discussion, action learning allows members to be accountable when they have not all the necessary information for the resolution of the problem . . . This experience is very interesting because [it] seizes an opening of the spirit, and the exchanges of opinions leads to a deeper analysis of the problem. It favors the spirit of group, of the team, collaboration, adds an exercise of the spirit of analysis and the spirit of criticizing [challenging] the members of the group. Action learning allows one to have confidence in self and to reduce the anxiety that one could have during the resolution of a real problem. Action learning reduces the risk of error (to divert oneself from the problem) because the group always has someone to return members to the posed problem although there is no one to lead the discussion. This freedom of expression! It is necessary to note that it is a major point [a major source of set energy]. When the discussion touches an element that retains the attention of the group, one finishes by feeling engaged; and therefore one wants to propose solutions to solve the personal problem, so the engagement is

strong. When the group marks a silence to seek the ideas and when one poses a question that re-launches the debate, one feels again more implicated and that allows one to be affirmed. At the same time that action learning redefines the problem . . . it allows the hidden aspects of the problem to be exposed and to propose a variety of solutions with the result that the problem holder . . . feels the joy. With solutions proposed in the form of questions, the problem holder has the feeling of being a "hero" satisfied with "his" work because the multitude of solutions gives him confidence to make a decision.

Willis, who worked with this group, believes that the reflective essays submitted (some translated from French) provide further evidence of the effectiveness of action learning in non-Western cultures. The comments cited are among many that exemplify the transformative nature of set activity for the African set members and for their client (the problem holder) who in this case was also a member of the set. During a reflective period at the conclusion of all set activity, the action learners were invited to draw pictures of action learning as they experienced it. Some drew pictures of meadows with plants growing at different heights, and all were blooming. Others drew pictures of groups of people holding hands in either a circle or a straight line as a gesture of unity. One drew a picture that was especially illustrative of tribal society: a village with huts at all four corners, with a single, unshaded light bulb in the center. Everyone in the village had a hand on or was eagerly reaching for the light bulb that was action learning.

Story 4

This is a story compiled from comments of various clients in a single organization regarding changed client perspectives and behaviors. In each case, the set members were masters-level graduate HRD students and the client was at either director or product manager level. All sets were single problem sets and no facilitator was present. The client specified the problem and then watched and participated also as a set member while the problem migrated and inquiry deepened. Three weeks into the process, Willis contacted each client individually and asked if things were going well, whether any problems had arisen, and what their impressions were at this point. Here is a sampling of their e-mailed responses:

> **Response 1.** I can already tell you that I have benefited tremendously from this experience. I have thoroughly enjoyed everyone in my group. They are the greatest. I also hope I have been able to shed some light on real-world experiences within corporate America. They [the students] have given me homework [data gathering] assignments and they are making me think. Sometimes I believe it is difficult to see the forest for the trees from where I sit—I feel very special to have been able to participate in the action learning program. (a director)
>
> **Response 2.** I'm very impressed with how quickly they are grasping the concept of my "issue" . . . Their good questions have already generated many things for me to think about . . . I look forward to our next meeting. (a product manager)
>
> **Response 3.** Everything is going well. They have been fun, energetic and really coming up with some unique questions. We brought my trainer into the meeting last week . . . I have been able to come up with some small solutions for now and have implemented some of them. I have some more ideas and just need a few more weeks to see if I can make it happen. It's been enjoyable and well worth the time so far. (a manager)

What is interesting about these client comments is (1) how early in the process the clients are reporting changes in their own thinking and actions, (2) how engaged they are in the process, and (3) how anticipation of more learning and insights yet to come propels them forward with action learning despite what they elsewhere described as heavy work loads and incredible time pressures. The same kinds of experiences propel the graduate student set members, most of whom are employed full time and go to evening classes. Although student comments are not reported above, they too sacrifice scarce leisure time to participate in the sets after working hours.

At the conclusion of the action learning period when set members present formally to their clients, the clients have confidently affirmed the utility of the process and the remarkable amount they have learned about themselves, their own work, and their organization. In the end, they consider the weekly action learning set meetings time efficient, for they have learned new strategies for tackling new problems in less time than they might have spent on a much less individualized two-day management seminar.

Perspective change is evident. One client was amused by the about-face in her expectations as she moved through the Alpha, Beta, and Gamma elements of the set activity. She said she had expected to be "a good citizen," doing corporate outreach by "teaching" the students about her work world. Instead, she said, she soon discovered that *she* was the principal learner.

SIGNS OF TRANSFORMATION

No doubt each individual in an active action learning set feels like the principal learner. While each set member is aware that others are seeing the world with new eyes, the changes in one's own point of view is most absorbing. Self-efficacy begins to be owned by those who have previously had no sense of being able to influence events and who have despaired of having a voice even in the decisions that affect them personally. For those generally confident, there are nevertheless incremental gains in willingness to try the untried and to take additional risks.

Revans noted "three cardinal features of action learning: enhanced interpersonal understanding, increased self-awareness, and economic insight" (Barker, 2000, p. 11). All these occurred in each of the stories told in this chapter, as in many other stories we might have told if time and space permitted. A great weight of evidence exists in participants' own words, to show that either changes by accretion or changes of the dramatic, turnaround kind are constantly occurring in action learning. Economic insights come in many shapes and forms, from understanding a little better why a "clever" work process may cost more than it saves, to understanding how national economies depend on ethical behaviors toward other nations.

Mezirow's transformative learning theory recognizes that transformations may build gradually over time or may arrive suddenly and dramatically as a result of some triggering incident. Going back to school, going abroad, moving to a new city, attending family events: such possible triggers for transformation are everywhere. Transformative learning is "centrally concerned with the structure and process of construal, validity testing, and reorganization of meaning" (Mezirow, 1991, p.7).

While meaning-making is highly individual, engaging in learning in a community of other learners provides incentives and models for new thinking. Action learning insists that action must be taken, but action, too, must be meaningful. Set members develop more flexible and systemic thinking styles because they have to, in order to interact successfully with people unlike themselves in contexts unlike those they usually inhabit. Being a set member engages the rational and the emotional simultaneously and naturally, thus opening up broad avenues for learning.

OTHER EVIDENCE OF CHANGED PERSPECTIVES

An Immediate "Go and Do It" Application

One action learner went from her set back to her own academic institution after a six-week trial of this new way to approach organizational change and immediately began to form in-house, cross-functional action learning sets. Their task was to tackle several recalcitrant problems connected with student admissions and new student advisement. The outcomes were (1) processing of student applications and administration of files were combined in one streamlined area, (2) new positions were created, (3) transcript evaluation was shifted to another department for greater efficiency, and (4) the changes set administrative standards for the opening of a satellite campus. Reflecting on her experience, this novice and new advocate of action learning said,

> Action learning opens up doors and allows tacit knowledge to spring forth from people. Fresh questions bring out ideas not exposed before . . . Professionally, it has brought education into the loop of problem solving. The focus is on learning, not just resolving. I have integrated it into my teams . . . There may be no such thing as an "expert in action learning" [because every group is different and] you can only understand and learn the process by doing it. (Willis, 1998, p. 504)

Imaging New Learning: Use of Metaphor

We have noticed over and over that action learning participants produce an extraordinary amount of metaphoric expression in connection with their struggle to accommodate to a learning experience unlike previous ones. These expressions may not always make it past the cutting floor of their reflective essays (we don't ask to see their journals) but they do pop out in conversations. Here are two out of many that did survive and appear in essays.

> **Example 1.** [Our] action learning group became one—not in the sense that it merged into a lifelong marriage, but in the sense that it truly engaged during the Spring 2001, as a team. The term that best describes the [set] was "blend." We were a blend of different individuals of different genders, ethnicity, ages, and learning styles with the task to solve a continuous learning problem . . . Yes, we were a blend. Yet what we were was really unimportant in comparison to what we became. Metaphorically speaking, we became a blend of fine tobaccos in an expensive Cuban cigar. We became a blend of exquisite Swiss chocolates in a

fine mocha coffee. We became a blend of high-performance fuel additives for the engine of a winning Indianapolis Speedway racecar.

Example 2. This semester has been quite a roller coaster ride . . . The action learning set meetings have contributed a lot to this ride. It also seemed as though I was playing Red Light, Green Light, go or whoa with this set as well. . . . The first night was a Green Light; we met with our [company] representative and we kicked things off at full speed . . . It was awesome . . . I thought I would solve [the problem] just for myself. Little did I know what lay ahead for me . . . [At Yellow Light] I am now drowning in overkill of information that doesn't seem pertinent to the situation at hand. I leave this meeting feeling empty . . . [Next meeting] we spoke to [the client] about the concept of action learning again and things started to look up. She started to answer our questions with some thought behind them and she even provided us with some homework we gave her. [Green Light]. Then hit the brakes, this statement [from the client] made my shoulders start to tense: "I want you to tell me what is best." Now it's back to reintroducing our role in the action learning set. That went over pretty well; I now do believe she has it. But my shoulders are still in a knot. . . . This has definitely been an experience like no other that I'm sure I will see again [but] all in all it was an experience I'm glad I had.

Wyatt supports our view that the metaphors action learners use merit our full attention, for "If we want to grasp the actuality of experience, we have to grant absolute relevance to the allusive and metaphoric quality of so much of our thinking . . ." (1967, p. 300).

Changing Perspectives Through Journaling

Lukinsky has written about the value adults add to their lives through journaling, when they discover it is a way to connect reflection and action (1990, p. 213). The gains in understanding that action learning participants make through reflective withdrawal and reentry, are constantly a theme in their essays. Two examples will serve.

> **Example 1.** I must admit that this is the first class in which I kept a true learning journal. I started the first night typing my thoughts, impressions, and reflections on the computer. I think it is interesting to see the transition in my writings as the course progressed. Ideas/thoughts came to me at times that were not conducive to writing them on the computer. During these times, I jotted them on post-it notes. One of these moments came to me while I was reading the text in the library. In my reflection I noted that as I progressed through the text, I found myself becoming more reflective. (Note: Of my set, I scored lowest on reflection.) I discovered that I asked myself more questions, Some unanswerable. Others demanding further reflection and inquiry—not just about the project, but how the group functioned and my role as set member.
>
> **Example 2.** I was pleasantly surprised at some of my thoughts and insight when I did take time to reflect, All of us seemed to slip into advice giving as we learned more about the problem. It was difficult not to want to offer suggestions. In reviewing my journal, I mentioned how difficult the problem was on several occasions and wondered if there was a solution or an answer. I recall being very frustrated in the third session . . . After this session, I wrote about how burned out I felt with graduate school . . . The more I learn, the more I realize how much more I have to learn . . . I can truly say that I have a thirst for knowledge that I did not realize before.

Self-Organizing in Absence of Leader Control

It has become very clear that, although participants initially feel shaky about being given real and consequential responsibility without the reassuring presence of a facilitator or a designated leader, they come to recognize how rapidly it builds self-confidence and the ability to function on their own. We have gathered dozens of pieces of evidence like the following:

> **Example 1.** I really appreciated the facilitator's support. Even though he never participated directly, we knew we could count on him and that he trusted us. He left us free to develop our project, but he was always there to answer any question or doubt. We were really glad by the end of the presentation [to the client] because we knew we met his expectations.
>
> **Example 2.** In our process, the role of the facilitator seemed to be unnecessary as we had no conflict we could not resolve or any problems with our client. On the contrary, the facilitator ensured we were on task ... He made us comfortable with the process and comfortable with our abilities to be successful in the process.
>
> **Example 3.** When I first arrived in this course I came in with the impression that it would be one of the easiest courses in the HRD curriculum. After the end of our first class, this notion was quickly expelled. The irony of action learning is that although you do not own the problem, your mind and body do not come to that realization ... I would find myself thinking about solutions to the problem at all hours of the day. Thus, the action learning project itself became one of the most rigorous experiences in the HRD program.

SUMMARY

There is literally no way in one chapter to catalogue the variety, range, and depth of the transformative learning experiences participants have written about. Perhaps one action learner from another Spring 2001 class has said it all: "WOW! What a process! What a challenge! What a learning experience!" Not all have experienced a major life change, as the woman in the first story did. But there is no doubt that at the very least, our students have made dramatic revisions in what they understand learning to be.

Trying to specify or individualize the outcomes of action learning before the process unfolds is like prescribing medicine before diagnosis. Prescriptive learning belongs only to the P in Revans's learning equation, and it is in the inquiring Q that the wealth of learning lies. This does not mean that all expectations are banned from consideration. It is the unfolding process itself that consistently tells us that individuals will be changed, why they will be changed, and to some extent at what points they are likely to be changed.

It is fruitless to try to predict exactly *what* a set member will know or be able to do as a result of engaging in action learning. We do know that insightful, meaningful, transformational learning manifests itself repeatedly—set by set, participant by participant. Some who undertake it are more ready than others to benefit from action learning. Some organizations are more ready than others to allow it to take place. And some learners are more articulate than others in describing changed views, beliefs, and behaviors. Despite these variables, it remains indisputable in our research findings that everyone who enters an action learning set takes away learning that adds value to past, present, and future. That learning can be retrieved more readily than if it were stored in P alone. As one learner expressed it, "Practice replaced theory and the abstract became concrete." We would add that, knowingly or not, learners were continuously crafting exciting new theories of life, learning, and action for themselves.

CHAPTER 8

Reflections on How To Bring It All Together

Action learning is not new; like all organic growth, it depends more upon the reinterpretation of old and familiar ideas than upon the acquisition of new cognitive knowledge.
— Reginald W. Revans (1983, p. 10)

The clever man will tell you what he knows; he may even try to explain it to you. The wise man encourages you to discover it for yourself, even though he knows it inside out. But since he seems to give you nothing, you have no need to reward him. Thus, the wise have disappeared and we are left in a desolation of the clever.
— Reginald W. Revans (1980, p. 9)

After reports about all the facts have reached their desks, after all the advice has been offered, all the opinions listened to, after everything has been listed for the final plan and the most talkative of experts is on the way back to the airport deciding in advance what he is going to tell his next client, the manager still remains alone with his responsibilities: he is the man who has to get something done.
— Reginald W. Revans (1983, p. 50)

Action learning is the Aristotelian manifestation of all managers' jobs: they learn as they manage, and they manage because they have learned—and go on learning.
— Reginald W. Revans (1983, p. 49)

Reflections on How To Bring It All Together

Action learning, as a concept, can take some getting used to, especially when it plays out in full alignment with the philosophy articulated by Revans. Having people assigned to solve problems outside their expertise can seem like setting out to have the blind lead the blind. It also flies in the face of the tightly orchestrated curricula, exemplified by classroom instruction and lecture, that we have been brought up to accept as the standard.

As a concept, action learning has been around for over 50 years, but until quite recently, its inroads as a vehicle for adult education and human resource development were limited. There was really no sense of urgency to try different techniques. Things began to change in the mid-1980s, characterized by a growing appreciation that established training programs were often failing to deliver results that matched expectations. Then in 1990, advanced by Senge's book *The Fifth Discipline* and others writing about creating the learning organization, attention began to shift to learning, as opposed to training or, for that matter, teaching.

Influencing this shift to a learning focus (e.g., continuous learning and lifelong learning) were the cataclysmic events related to the global marketplace. Suddenly, the envelope of competition expanded to include the entire world, not just the U.S. economy or competition in El Paso, Miami, or Peoria. Now the competition was with workers and industries in Taipei, Bangkok, Dublin, and Iwacuni, Japan. It ushered in the era of continuous restructuring and need to continually run faster and faster to just stay in place, let alone advance. The pressure was felt organizationally and individually. Workers found that their livelihoods hinged on continuing to grow professionally, gaining new competencies as markets and technologies shifted.

All of the turbulence in the world markets turned attention in the direction of performance and cultural transformation (i.e., remolding the thought processes and belief systems undergirding how you organize and manage a business) in order to survive and prosper. Companies like GE, that showed the way in accomplishing such a paradigm shift, became the role model for others.

The desire for high-performing workplaces caused organizations to turn away from the more traditional approaches to education and HRD and toward innovative ways of creating high-performance learning cultures. This opened up an avenue for action learning as a way to promote real-time learning that is immediately usable, build the long-term capacity of the human resource base, and both develop and sustain high performance.

Use of action learning today ranges from the timid (limited application) to the robust (full application) approach. In the timid approach, there can be more form than substance. It can even be a traditional task force under a new name, with little consideration of the all important learning component. Tasks are often selected by the learner. That matches with the learner centeredness of andragogy, but it can lead to selection of lower priority, less risky (even "safe") projects. In a robust application on the other hand the projects to be worked on are of major importance to the organization and can be directly related to strategic goals and vision of the enterprise.

What follows are frames of reference that can be helpful in inaugurating an action learning program.

CONTINUUM FOR ACTION LEARNING INITIATIVES

TIMID ←————————→ ROBUST

Limited Application

- Stay with formal learning programs, including a few narrow opportunities for action learning.
- Let participants select/negotiate a project without

Full Application

- Empower teams/action learning sets to work on problems of highest priority to the organization.
- Give strong emphasis to balancing action and reflection.

regard to what carries the highest priority in the organization.
- Continue to use task forces in trouble-shooting major issues/problems, but without any significant address of the learning component, including reflection on learning.
- Know that there is limited (and even uninformed) top management support.

- Assign projects to teams that are unfamiliar, complex and in the unsolvable range.
- Give the team wide license to be innovative and challenge established ways of doing business.
- Know that top management fully understands and supports.

SELECTION OF ACTION LEARNING MODEL

Joint Project

- Pick one of the major challenges facing the organization, linked to strategic priorities.
- If appropriate, use an established self-directed work team or natural team, assigning them a problem with which they are unfamiliar.
- At the outset, consider assigning the set an open-ended requirement, such as proposals for improving the organization (similar to what GE did initially with its workouts).

Everyone Bring One (EBO) Project

- Consider assigning an individual project that is critical and begs for a solution. (It can be with the person's organization or a different one, as occurred in the Belgian model.)
- Make sure that individual projects have relative parity in terms of complexity.
- Strive to assign projects that are outside the specific expertise of the person.

DETERMINING ACTION LEARNING SET COMPOSITION

Do's

- Use action learning as a way of building networks and integrating the enterprise by creating cross-functional sets.
- Go for diversity of perspectives by managing who is in a set. (Consider as a minimum the following balances: gender, ethnicity/nationality, professional background, learning style differences, age, and personalities.)
- Understand that set members should usually be at the same level in the organization, especially in multinational/multicultural sets.
- Mix organizational levels, if appropriate, in the interest of opening up cross-hierarchical communications and emphasizing the importance of everyone in organization to corporate success. (This approach can mean lowering the difficulty of the project so it is not beyond the reach of those less experienced.)
- Designate the set a person will be assigned to in order to balance quality across multiple sets.

Don'ts

- Don't place a group of like-thinking associates in a set.
- Don't let people choose which set they belong to. That can create cliques and unbalance the relative capability of multiple sets (some weak and some strong).
- Don't determine set composition at random. (You want to purposely engineer set composition to create an effective learning community).

IDENTIFYING A SUITABLE PROJECT

Do's

- Scope the project carefully (unsolved, complex, do-able in time available, solid host support likely).
- Make sure you know who the clients are. (It is almost always multiple.)
- Realize that clients need to have the authority to implement set recommendations. (That usually also means, by deductive reasoning, that the specific client needs the support of top management.)
- Understand the specific context (e.g., a community college in rural Virginia) and the organizational culture. Organizational culture, if rigid and set against change, can defeat even the most genuine project offer by the client.
- Determine the potential learning value of one project versus another.
- Consider whether the overall intellectual level and maturity level of the set (not specific expertise) properly fits with the level of challenge.

Don'ts

- Don't select a project casually (the first one that drops in your lap) and expect it all to work out somehow.
- Don't assume you understand what the clients are after, or the kind of support they can deliver to the set. This needs to be clearly laid down in a memorandum of understanding.

MEMORANDUM OF UNDERSTANDING

The memorandum of understanding with the client should include the following points.

- What each party expects of the other in terms of bringing the project to fruition.
- A clear statement by the client of what the problem is, how it manifests itself, and what the desired end state is (that is, what ought to be happening).
- Agreement on when the final product is to be delivered and what it is specifically to encompass.
- Who the set should contact when it needs additional information/data.
- How rapidly the organization will respond to set questions and requests for information (for example, 48 to 72 hours).
- The date when the relationship will terminate.
- Any understandings concerning the resources the set will need from the organization in accomplishing its work.

PRINCIPAL PITFALLS TO AVOID AND POSSIBLE REMEDIES

Pitfalls	Remedies
• The agreement with the client is fuzzy.	• Don't enter the relationship until a definitive memorandum of understanding has been struck.
• Top management support is lacking in the host/client organization.	• Top management should actively support the initiative if there is to be a reasonable chance of a successful project diagnosis and follow-on implementation. This needs to be a part of the up-front

- Client fails to deliver on promises and commitments made.

- Set members cannot seem to get along with one another.

- Set members complain of high stress levels.

- The action component drives out the reflective component.

negotiation with the client firm.
- Client lives in a real, rough and tumble world, and unexpected events may intrude on the ability to be fully responsive at times. If it is not possible to ride through the interruption of support, the memorandum of understanding will need to be renegotiated, or in the very worst case, the agreement may need to be terminated.
- Allow the set to try and work it out, with perhaps some general guidance from the learning coach. If that fails, the learning coach may need to intervene and move through a conflict resolution process.
- Stress tends to be self-imposed. The learning coach should work with the set in identifying sources of stress and how to ameliorate them if the set cannot work through it on its own. This is the first choice because of what can be learned by an intra-set review of what is happening.
- This is a common problem. The United States is an activist society, and participants will tend to be achieve-

- The set receives pressure from those in the organization, other than the client, to stay away from given areas deemed to be politically sensitive.

ment driven. The reflective component needs to be emphasized from the beginning. The keeping of learning logs/journals by the participants along the way can be of help. Encourage the set to put time aside for reflection. The learning coach can plan some time in meeting with the set to promote reflection and discuss learning goals/yields. The learning coach can, in the case of multiple sets, arrange an exchange of set members through the creation of hybrid (combined) sets, with the entire focus on learning and group reflection.

- The client should be asked to run interference for the set in such cases. It is not the set's job to deal with the internal politics of the client firm. The prospect of such an issue should be surfaced when the memorandum of understanding is negotiated. The client should be in a position to deal with such issues if there is to be a reasonable expectation that recommendations made by the set will be implemented.

- Recommendations are approved by the client, but implementation seems doubtful.

- A truly viable action learning program takes this into account from the begin-

Reflections on How To Bring It All Together 181

	ning of the project. The implementation machinery needs to be understood and geared up so that the baton can be passed smoothly between the set and whomever (e.g., a follow-on set) is to implement the recommendations. This can be made a part of the memorandum of understanding and such inclusion is recommended.
• Set receives continuous heat from the training department in the organization because it sees action learning as a threat.	• This needs to be part of the basic scoping going in. If the human resources department is going to be an opponent, it must be neutralized. That can be done by bringing department members on board (persuading them of the value and allaying their fears) or by sufficient clout on the part of the client and top management to block or defeat such a challenge.
• Employees of the organization refuse to participate in action learning.	• While volunteerism is the goal, the action learning initiative is really no different than any other human resource development initiative in the organization. There are some basic human resource development strategies that must be honored. GE could not be expected to make its work-outs, change acceleration or Six Sigma initiatives permissive. Each

is a core driver in building the culture and capabilities needed for long-term success. The same is true of action learning. The client and top management must stand behind the effort in ensuring participation.

LEARNING COACH ROLES

Role/Rationale	Assessment
Role 1: The learning coach is always or usually present when the set meets. • The learning coach needs to assist in guiding the learning process. • The learning coach needs to see what is happening. • "What role would I have if I'm not present?" asks the learning coach.	This works against andragogy (adult learning theory) by fostering dependency on an authority figure. The presence of a learning coach changes the fundamental group dynamics. The learning coach is *not* a set member.
Role 2: The learning coach is always present but only speaks if the set requests assistance or advice. • The learning coach can oversee. • The learning coach is available immediately if a problem arises.	Having the learning coach in the room is not a benign presence. It tends to alter basic group dynamics and subtly promotes learner dependency. What is said is not exactly what would be said if the learning coach were not present (i.e., there will be posturing that occurs).

Role 3:
The learning coach is present only by prearrangement (e.g., to discuss learning process) or by an invitation to enter the set environment.
- Adults should be treated as adults.
- Set members are their own best facilitators of learning (Revans).
- A significant part of the learning (e.g., conflict resolution) comes from the struggle and the learning coach should only intervene in the most urgent cases.

This most closely conforms to the andragogical model and action learning philosophy of Reg Revans. Learners need to be emancipated from the confining structures prevalent in traditional classroom approaches if they are to transform themselves and help move their organizations to a higher performance plateau.

SUMMARY

We live in a dynamic time where even recent conceptions of learning in relation to performance are being questioned. For example, much has been written about workplace learning. Where is the workplace in an increasingly virtual world? There has also been a heavy emphasis on transfer of learning, in part a carryover from an age when most learning occurred in a classroom and then was to be practiced in the workplace. The question is whether what is learned finds its way into the workplace in terms of measurable performance improvement.

In action learning, where you work directly on a real issue of importance, the transfer of learning emphasis loses force. The problem solution and the learning tend to be concurrent and conjoined, so close is the interweave. An employee who calls up a tutorial on a computer screen to deal with a problem of that moment is learning, but are we looking at transfer of learning? As we move from classroom-based instruction to the fluidity of

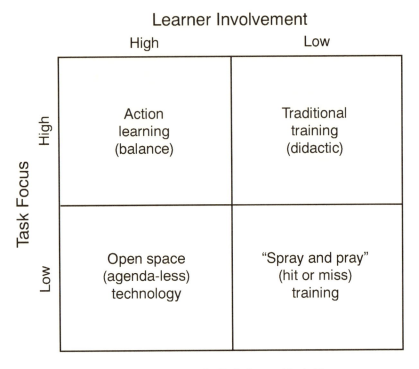

Figure 8.1 Learner Involvement in Relation to Task Focus

action and learning intertwined, frames of reference like transfer of learning take on new meaning. They can even begin to become dysfunctional at least for the growing segment of the learning process that is experiential in nature.

Figure 8.1 depicts learner involvement in relation to task focus in comparing several learning approaches.

What one comes away with after exploring action learning in a comprehensive way, as we have tried to do in this book, is an appreciation for the robustness of the modality. It is not for the faint of heart or those organizations that are risk averse. Unlike traditional curricula, it does not have a predictable outcome, even though usually successful. Learning goals are not preordained. The learning yields shape themselves as the action learning process unfolds. Learners take control of their own learning.

While action learning can appear to lack structure, it in fact has self-ordering properties. The process guides the experience. It ends up being a disciplined process because the learners bring order to it in adapting it to the challenges being faced and exigencies encountered. It is that kind of ready adaptability that the dynamics of the emerging workplace require. Action learning has a high performance thrust to it and it is high performance that organizations seek, with a concomitant understanding that competitive advantage centers on the quality of the continuous learning that takes place.

Action learning as outlined by Revans has three systems associated with it that are interlocking. System Alpha provides the initial picture frame, with its three fundamental questions:

1. What is happening?

2. What ought to be happening?

3. What do we need to do to make it happen?

System Beta covers five areas:

1. Survey or observation.

2. Hypothesis or theory.

3. Experiment or test.

4. Audit or evaluation.

5. Review or ratification.

System Beta is easily identifiable when you review the steps in the action learning process addressed in Chapter 5.

System Gamma is the transformative piece, where the learning process of the action learning participant and the systems of the client organization undergo symbiotic change. The learner can escape defensive attitudes, become a better listener, grow in personal maturity, and learn to change behavior by in-depth reflection and address of underlying assumptions that have guided behavior.

In the end, action learning has an authenticity about it in terms of honest communication, empathy for others, and the ability to see reality through a clearer self-image and environmental lens. The congruence of so many explicit and implicit benefit yields makes action learning an increasingly popular intervention in the pursuit of high-performance organizations and healthy workplaces.

GLOSSARY

Action. The centerpiece of action learning is action, in that the experience is to lead to action. As Reg Revans states, there is no learning without action and no action without learning. The action/project serves as the engine that drives the process, promoting learning and critical reflection.

Action learning. Action learning is a process of reflecting on one's work and beliefs in a supportive/confrontational environment of one's peers for the purpose of gaining new insights and resolving real business and community problems in real time.

Action learning set. A group of four to eight individuals selected to participate in an action learning experience. There is no assigned leader within the team. All members of the set enjoy equal status. Revans considers five to be the ideal set size.

Action Learning Team Process Questionnaire (ALTPQ). An instrument developed by John Bing of ITAP International and Robert Dilworth of Virginia Commonwealth University to monitor the internal action learning set group dynamics as seen through the eyes of its members (i.e., perceptions). Positives and negatives related to the action learning experience are also plotted.

Belgian project. An action learning program conducted in Belgium in the 1960s on a national scale. Developed and orchestrated by Reg Revans, action learning's principal pioneer, it involved action learning sets of five senior corporate executives, each dealing with a major problem area that was outside the bounds of their prior business experience, as they shared with their set colleagues concerns and insights on the learning taking place.

Client. The person or person who will be relating to the action learning set or individual members (depending on the action learning model used) in refining the problem in the client organization and receiving the results of the action learning effort.

Critical reflection. The purposeful effort to reflect on one's experiences in depth in order to reveal the underlying assumptions that govern our lives and perceptions of the world. In action learning this is done both individually and in collective dialogue within the action learning set.

Everyone Bring One (EBO) model. This is an action learning set in which each member brings a different problem to the table, usually from that member's workplace.

Four squares. A model used by Reg Revans to demonstrate that problems we confront in our lives are either familiar or unfamiliar and occur in a familiar or unfamiliar setting. Revans argues that the greatest learning occurs when we find ourselves confronting an unfamiliar problem in an unfamiliar setting. We are then most inclined to ask fresh questions and challenge our own long-held assumptions.

Hybrid set. This is a term used when members of multiple sets are mixed together to form new sets for the purpose of broadening the exchange of views on learning that is taking place. By bringing a cross-section of sets together, the intense project focus tends to be temporarily diffused, elevating the likelihood that reflection on learning can occur.

Joint project model. This is an action learning set where all members are dealing with a common problem, usually of great complexity.

Learning coach. Also referred to as set advisor, advisor, facilitator, or mentor, the learning coach guides the action learning process, to include assistance in determining the appropriate project and arriving at set composition. The learning coach role can range from omnipresence in set meetings to an interruptive involvement based on need and invitation by the set to participate. Reg Revans believes in minimal facilitation and intervention by a learning coach.

Learning equation. Revans suggests that learning equals programmed knowledge, what he refers to as P, plus questioning insight, or the Q factor. He espouses the belief that while both the P and the Q are necessary for learning to occur, the P (formal and accrued learning) needs to be preceded by the Q and its free-ranging address of what is happening and needs to occur. In other words, the Q drives the P.

Programmed knowledge (P). This encompasses all the forms of formal/instrumental learning we are commonly exposed to, including lectures, textbooks, case studies, simulations, and puzzles. Revans states that all forms of programmed knowledge travel out of what has occurred in the past, and therefore represent imperfect formulations in dealing with problems that we either are facing now or might expect to face in the future.

Questioning insight (Q). The Q factor hinges on asking the right questions. Revans indicates that we need an added infusion of the Q factor in dealing with the times in which we live, since our capacity to learn is now often outstripped by the velocity of the change forces around us. Through questioning insight we are able to test the adequacy of available P and determine if it is flawed. In some cases, we will find it necessary to discount existing P and create new P. If we had started with the existing P rather than Q, we might have been inclined to accept P that would have led us in the wrong direction.

System Alpha. This is the first of three interlinked systems of thought and action in Revans's concept of action learning. It features iterative, evolving analysis of a real problem situation in its organizational context. During this process, unexpected roots and ramifications are bared. Novel attacks on problems can be mounted when action learners continually ask themselves the questions: What is happening? What ought to be happening? How can it be made to happen? The same questions will apply at different points throughout the inquiry. They are pivotal when obtaining an initial problem statement or when tracking the migration of that problem over time as new insights are obtained.

System Beta. This system resembles the use of the scientific method in the physical and life sciences. Revans calls it "intelligent trial and error." Beta elaborates on what is derived in System Alpha, applying fact-finding and assumption-testing procedures to check and double check what is being learned. System Beta includes field research, data collection and interpretation, and other discovery methods (such as those described in the Action Learning Phase in Chapter 5.) Survey and/or observation, trial hypothesis or theory, experiment (test), audit (evaluation), and review, ratification, or rejection of results are all necessary Beta processes. System Beta uses whatever is revealed to pursue new avenues of inquiry that might yield a better solution.

System Gamma. This system, grounded in critical reflection, is embedded in all the action learning processes. Revans calls it "symbiotic" with Alpha and Beta. It demands an honest search for understanding of the realities and value systems of self and others, since it is these realities and values that guide what people say and do. Revans insists that greater self-knowledge leads to greater interpersonal competence and more sensitive organizational skills. System Gamma, with the transformational change opportunities it offers, is the very core of action learning and the energy source for its powerful effects.

Transformative learning. We are transformed to the extent we are able to either modify or jettison assumptions that are revealed as no longer having meaning, replacing them with new and more fully differentiated points of view and frames of reference. Learning in and of itself contains the seeds of transformation. When we learn, we are transformed.

Virtual organization/Virtuality. Action learning in a virtual mode involves doing most, if not all, of the set business/interaction by teleconference, e-mail or other electronic means, as opposed to face-to-face interaction. This provides special challenges to a modality predicated on intimate, direct, and regular face-to-face contact where all the senses are engaged. The challenge is further magnified when dealing cross-culturally with global teams. This is relatively unexplored ground with respect to action learning.

REFERENCES

Argyris, C., Putnam, R., & Smith, D. (1985). *Action science*. San Francisco: Jossey-Bass.

Barker, A. (1998). Profile of action learning's principal pioneer — Reginald W. Revans. *Performance Improvement Quarterly, 11*(1), 9–22.

Barker, A. (2000). *In pursuit of System Gamma*. Unpublished manuscript made available to authors.

Canadian Centre for Management Development (CCMD) Report No. 1 (1999). *Continuous Learning*. A CCMD Publication.

Casey, D. & Pearce, D. (eds.). (1977). *More than management development: Action learning at GEC*. AMACOM and Farnborough, UK: Teakfield, Ltd.

Colky, D. L., Colky, M. T., & Young, W. H., III. (2002). Managing and developing people in the virtual organization. Malabar, FL: Krieger.

Daloz, L. A. P., Keen, C. H., Keen, J. P. & Parks, S. D. (1996). *Common fire*. Boston: Beacon Press.

Dilworth, R. L. (1998). Action learning in a nutshell. *Performance Improvement Quarterly, 11*(1), 28–43.

Dilworth, R. L., Willis, V. J., & Barker, A. E. (1998). *Characteristics of action learning*. Unpublished manuscript.

Gilley, J. & Maycunich (1998). *Strategically integrated HRD*. Reading, MA: Addison-Wesley.

Goldberg, M. (1998). *The art of the question*. New York: John Wiley & Sons.

Hall, C. S. & Lindzey, G. (1970). *Theories of personality*. New York: John Wiley & Sons.

Handy, C. (1996). *The search for meaning*. London: Lemos & Crane.

Hawkins, H. (1995). *Strange attractors*. New York: Prentice Hall (Harvester Wheatshop).

Hofstede, G. (1984). *Culture's consequences*. Newbury Park: Sage.

Inglis, S. (1994). *Making the most of action learning.* Aldershot, UK: Gower.

Introducing the MIL international newsletter and reporting from the EFMD annual conference 1994—the special event at MIL campus (1996). Copy editor, *MIL Concepts 1,* 4–5.

Kennedy, W. B. (1990). Integrating personal and social ideologies. In Mezirow & Associates, *Fostering critical reflection in adulthood.* San Francisco: Jossey-Bass.

Knowles, M. (1990). *The adult learner* (4th ed.). Houston, TX: Gulf.

Kuhn, T. S. (1977). *The essential tension.* Chicago: University of Chicago Press.

Lanahan, E. D. & Maldonado, L. (1998). Accelerated decision making via action learning at the Federal Deposit Insurance Corporation (FDIC). *Performance Improvement Quarterly, 11* (1), 74–85.

Lindeman, E. (1961, 1926). *The meaning of adult education.* Norman, OK: Oklahoma Research Center for Continuing Professional and Higher Education.

Livingston, J. (1998). Pygmalion in Management. *Harvard Business Review,* 66-5, 121–130.

Lukinsky, J. (1990). Reflective withdrawal through journal writing. In Mezirow & Associates, *Fostering critical reflection in adulthood.* San Francisco: Jossey-Bass.

Marquardt, M. (1999). *Action learning in action.* Palo Alto, CA: Davies-Black.

Marsick, V. (1990). Action learning and reflection in the workplace. In Mezirow & Associates, *Fostering critical reflection in adulthood.* San Francisco: Jossey-Bass.

Marsick, V. & Cederholm, L. (1988). Developing leadership in international managers—an urgent challenge! *The Columbia Journal of World Business,* xxx111 (4), 1–9.

Meister, J. (1998). *Corporate universities.* New York: McGraw-Hill.

Mezirow, J. (1991). *Transformative dimensions of adult learning.* San Francisco: Jossey-Bass.

Mezirow, J. & Associates. (1990). *Fostering critical reflection in adulthood: A guide to transformative and emancipatory learning.* San Francisco: Jossey-Bass.

Morgan, G. (1989). *Creative organization theory: A resourcebook.* London: Sage.

Mulgan, G. (1997). *Connexity.* Boston: Harvard Business School Press.

Mumford, A. (1985). *Management Bibliographies and Reviews, 11* (2). Bradford, UK: MCB University Press.

Nee, E. (2001, July 23). Open season on Carly Fiorina. *Fortune, 144*(2), 115.
Pedler, M. (1991). *Action learning in practice* (2nd ed.). London: Gower.
Potts, M. (1990, October 7). Seeking a better way. *The Washington Post*, pp. H1, H4.
Revans, R. W. (1970). The managerial alphabet. In G. Heald (Ed.), *Approaches to the study of organizational behavior: Operations research and the behavioral sciences*, pp. 141–161. London: Tavistock Publications.
Revans, R. W. (1971). *Developing effective managers*. New York: Praeger.
Revans, R. W. (1972). *Culture M*. Unpublished manuscript (with two earlier drafts), Revans archives. Salford, UK: University of Salford Library.
Revans, R. W. (1980). *Action learning: New techniques for management*. London: Blond & Briggs.
Revans, R. W. (1982). *The origins and growth of action learning*. Bromley, UK: Chartwell-Bratt.
Revans, R. W. (1983). *ABC of action learning*. Bromley, Kent: Chartwell-Bratt.
Rohlin, T. (1996). What do we mean by action reflection learning. *MIL Concepts 1*, 1996, a newsletter of the Management Institute of Lund (MIL).
Rommel, E. (1979). *Attacks*. Vienna, VA: Athena Press, Inc.
Schein, E. (1997). *Three cultures of management: The key to organizational Learning in the 21st Century*. MIT Sloan School of Management.
Schön, D. (1983). *The reflective practitioner*. New York: Basic Books.
Schumacher, E. F. (1973). *Small is beautiful: A study of economics as if people mattered*. London: Blond & Briggs.
Senge, P. M. (1990). *The fifth discipline: Mastering the five practices of the learning organization*. New York: Doubleday.
Slater, R. (1993). *The new GE*. Homewood, IL: Business One Irwin.
Stewart, T. A. (1991, August 12). How Jack Welch keeps the ideas flowing. *Fortune*, 41–49.
Stogdill, R. M. (Ed.) (1970). *The process of model building in the behavioral sciences*. New York: Norton.
Tichy, N. M. & Sherman, S. (1993). *Control your own destiny or someone else will*. New York: Doubleday.
Tuckman, B. W. & Jensen, M. A. C. (1977, December). Stages of small group development revisited. *Group and Organization Studies, 2*(4), 419–427.

Weinstein, K. (1995). *Action learning: A journey into discovery and development*. London: Harper Collins.

Weisbord, M. (1987). *Productive workplaces*. San Francisco: Jossey-Bass.

Willis, V. J. (1998). Verifying themes in action learning: Implications for adult education and HRD. *Proceedings of the Academy of Human Resource Development*. Baton Rouge, LA: Academy of Human Resource Development and ERIC document.

Willis, V. J. (1999). *Overview of action learning*. Presentation to the Southeastern Society for Organizational Learning, Atlanta, Georgia, January 1999.

Willis, V. J. (2000, March). Searching for meaning in complex action learning data: What environments, acts, and words reveal. In K. P. Kuchinke, (Ed.), *Proceedings of the Academy of Human Resource Development*. Baton Rouge, LA: Academy of Human Resource Development and ERIC document.

Willis, V. J. & Dilworth, R. L. (2000, October). Transformative learning in an international action learning context: From the learner's perspective. In C. Weissner, S. R. Meyn, & D. A. Fuller (Eds.), *Challenges of practice: Transformative learning in action*. Third International Transformative Learning Conference, Columbia University. ERIC document.

Wyatt, F. (1967). Psychology and the humanities: A case of no-relationship. In J. F. T. Bugenthal (Ed.), *Challenges of humanistic psychology*, pp. 290–301. New York: McGraw-Hill.

Yorks, L., O'Neil, J., & Marsick, V. (1999). Action learning: Theoretical bases and varieties of practices. Monograph of the Academy of Human Resource Development on Action Learning.

INDEX

Academic domains, 36, 48, 49, 128, 166. *See also* Application domains
Academic settings. *See* Academic domains
Action, xi, 7, 11, 21, 32, 33, 42, 55, 75, 84, 125, 132, 153, 154, 156, 157, 161, 164, 166, 187
  balance with learning and reflection, xii, 7, 11, 21, 22, 92, 95, 131, 137, 138, 157, 169, 174, 179, 184, 187
  theories of action, 171. *See also* Espoused theory vs. theory-in-use
Action learning, 1, 5, 7, 10, 187
  acculturated, 56, 146
  basic principles, xv, 6, 15–17, 53, 56, 137, 187–190. *See also* Action learning theory and governing philosophy
  cardinal features, 165
  cascading effect, 31, 32
  catalytic value, xiii, 39, 53, 79, 155, 156
  characteristics. *See* Action learning characteristics
  compared to other interventions, 17, 27, 31–32, 64, 70–72
  complexity dimensions. *See* Complexity
  core, 6, 12–14
  definitions, 10–12
  origins, xv, 1, 2, 5–9
  power of, 1, 2, 7, 8, 9, 11, 56, 79, 161, 190
Action learning advocacy, 74, 132, 151, 167
Action Learning and Mutual Collaboration Congress. *See* Global aspects
Action learning characteristics, 12–14, 15, 71
Action learning checklists. *See* Frames of reference
Action learning contexts, 20, 36. *See also* Contexts
Action learning cycle and phases, 74, 77, 78, 102, 103, 112, 113, 120, 121. *See also* Action learning phase; Implementation phase; Initiation phase
Action learning debriefing, 69
Action learning descriptive terms
  approach to developing and managing people, xiv, 11, 29, 61, 67–70, 74
  change agent; change process, viii, xvi, 6, 11, 14, 15, 21,

25, 32, 33, 39, 57, 61, 103, 109, 113, 114, 116, 121, 122, 157, 170, 184
cross-disciplinary, 10, 15
eclectic, 10, 15, 31
egalitarian, 12, 22, 23, 31, 147, 156, 187
emergent, 40
face-to-face, 41, 49, 88, 140, 191
habit (for effective learning), xv
mosaic of elements, 15, 71, 79, 109
natural learning, xiii, 2, 11, 19, 30, 31, 35, 51, 54, 74, 95, 142, 147, 150, 166
organic growth, 172
product, 11, 89, 157, 178
purposeful, xii, 11, 54
repertoire, 51
robust, 184
sleeping giant, xi
spontaneous, xi, 45, 95
strategic (strategy for learning and change), xiii, 28, 30, 31, 54, 67, 86, 96
theory. *See* Action learning theory and governing philosophy
think tank, xi
transformative; transformation, xvi, 27. *See also* Transformative learning
Action learning distribution, vii, xv, 51, 69, 70, 137, 138, 153
Action learning domains of practice, xv, xvi, 36, 126–151. *See also* Application domains

Action learning equation, 15–17, 189
 P (programmed knowledge), vii, 12, 15–18, 32, 35, 40, 44, 53, 60, 76, 113, 114, 171, 189
 Q (questioning insight), vii, 12, 15–17, 32, 35, 40, 171, 189. *See also* Inquiry processes; Insights
Action learning facilitation, 13, 14, 15, 17, 21, 24, 25. *See also* Facilitation
Action learning four-squares model, 18–21. *See also* Familiar problems; Four squares; Unfamiliar problems
Action learning in a nutshell, 32
Action learning phase (in action learning cycle), 77, 112–119
Action learning presentations, 65, 66, 69, 80, 101, 119–121, 165, 170
 presentation audience, 119, 120
Action learning program design. *See* Action learning phase; Diversity by design; Implementation phase; Initiation phase; Set composition
Action learning project models, 78–84, 112, 113, 175
 Belgian project model, viii, 9, 76, 79, 81–84, 109, 112, 122, 123, 175, 187
 EBO (Everyone Bring One) model, 14, 78, 79, 80, 81, 84, 89, 98, 103, 112, 120,

Index

130, 161, 175, 188. *See also* Universities using action learning
Hybrid fourth model, 76, 83, 84, 89, 90, 112, 118, 122, 158
Joint project and EBO models compared, 71, 80, 84, 175
Joint project model, 14, 78, 79, 80, 81, 83, 84, 88, 89, 98, 103, 112, 114, 120, 122, 130, 131, 158, 163, 175, 188. *See also* Universities using action learning
Action learning set guidelines, xiii, 23, 88. *See also* Working team agreement
Action learning sets, 9, 13, 14, 19, 21-25, 31, 33, 39, 41, 47, 51, 55, 60, 65, 73, 76, 78-103, 108-124, 129, 130, 132, 133, 137, 142, 155-159, 162-169, 170, 171, 175-183, 187, 191. *See also* Set composition
Action Learning Team Process Questionnaire (ALTPQ), 96, 97, 187
Action learning theory and governing philosophy (Revans), xv, 5, 6, 8, 10, 12, 17, 19, 24, 63, 82, 122, 131, 173, 183
Action learning time frames, xvi, 32, 70, 88, 89, 91, 94, 103, 113, 118, 165, 178
Action-Reflection-Learning (ARL), 16, 17, 69, 70
Action research, xii, 7, 9
Action science, 7
Adaptability; adaptation, 1, 18, 19, 29, 30, 56, 62, 74, 75, 106, 126, 149, 160, 185
Adjunct, part-time faculty, 133, 134
Adult basic education, xxi, 36, 134-136
Adult education; adult educators, xv, xxi, 10, 25-28, 31, 36, 40, 51, 128, 129, 131-136, 139, 140, 173
Adult learning theory and principles, 2, 10, 15, 26, 35, 42, 60, 127, 133, 182
African set, 162, 163
Agenda setting; goal determination, 6, 8, 13, 27, 41, 42, 62, 65
Alliances (organizational and global), 153
American Society for Training and Development (ASTD), 145
Andragogy, 26, 27, 28, 120, 129, 133, 174, 182, 183
Anomaly, 67, 155
Application domains, 35, 36, 46, 126-151
 academic related, 36
 business, service related, 36
 government, 36
 system changers, 36
 world, 36
Argyris, C. and Schon, D., 72
Argyris, C., Putnam, R., and Smith, D., 72
Assumptions, 7, 13, 21, 27, 28, 31, 32, 33, 34, 37, 38, 40, 43, 45, 46, 48, 52, 53, 59, 69, 77, 83, 90, 97, 105, 119, 123, 127, 144, 150, 151, 157, 188, 190

dominant, xvi, 38
four common, 38, 43, 45, 47–51, 127, 150. *See also* Curriculum dominance; Leader control of learning; Learning guarantees; Learning on the fly
Authenticity of action learners and learning, 55, 72, 160, 185

Balance of action and reflection. *See* Action
Barker, A., 8, 12, 15, 160, 165
Barriers to action learning, 43, 46, 48, 49, 54, 60, 62, 72, 96, 126. *See also* Assumptions; Biases; Implementation
Baughman, J., 63, 64
Belgian project, 9, 76, 109, 122, 123, 187. *See also* Action learning project models
Beliefs; belief systems, 11, 33, 35, 46, 53, 55, 69, 72, 97, 106, 121, 123, 126, 171, 173. *See also* Authenticity of action learners and learning; Value systems
Belittlement of subordinates, 43, 47
Best practices, 69, 100, 127, 144
Biases, 34, 41, 42, 53. *See also* Assumptions, four common
context-fed, xv, 37, 38, 40
discipline-based, xv. *See also* Contexts; Cultures; Disciplines
Bicycle analogy, ix
Bing, J., 187

Bonding, 52, 80, 115, 137, 141. *See also* Set cohesion and continuity
Boundary openness, 22, 31, 56, 62, 64, 85
Breakthrough thinking, 16, 157, 160
Briggs and Peat, *Turbulent Mirrors*, 155
Bureaucracy, 50, 61, 63, 64, 144
Businesses and related services, 36, 48, 49, 71, 136. *See also* Application domains

Canadian Center for Management Development (CCMD), 13, 126
Capacities; capabilities, xiv, 85, 138, 145, 148, 149, 174, 182. *See also* Organizational development and change; Organizational learning; Personal growth
Capstone course design features, xv. *See also* Action learning cycle and phases
Casey, D. and Pearce, D., 85
Cavendish Laboratories, 8
Challenges, xiv, 52, 57, 59, 79, 80, 81, 89, 102, 127, 132, 134, 137, 139, 151, 170, 177, 191. *See also* Action learning presentations; Comfort zones; Commitment; Reflection
Championed decisions, 67. *See also* Power
Championing of change, 62, 63, 68, 76
Chaos theory, 155

Characteristics of action learning. *See* Action learning characteristics
Charismatic influences of successful leaders, 43, 47
Checklists, xvi. *See also* Frames of reference
Chief executive officer (CEO), 58, 62, 67, 73, 75, 106, 128, 142
Chief knowledge officer (CKO), 149
Chief learning officer (CLO), xxii, 36, 140, 149–151. *See also* System changers
Chief training officer, 102, 150
City of Hampton, 145
Cleverness, viii, 7, 166, 172
Client, 14, 76, 78, 102, 103, 120, 158, 179, 180, 188. *See also* Participation
client scoping, 110, 111, 117
Climate, organizational, 72, 106, 107
Coal miners, 8, 19, 20
Colky, Colky and Young, 140
Collaborative inquiry. *See also* Inquiry processes
Comfort zones, 35
  anxiety avoidance, 12
  disorienting, triggering events, 155, 159, 166
  outside of comfort zone or expertise, 32
Commitment, xii, xvi, 13, 33, 37, 54, 57, 62, 67, 80, 82, 83, 92, 161, 179
Common good, 154, 156
Commons (village), 153–155
Communication, 35, 58, 141, 142, 176. *See also* Inquiry processes
Communities, xii, xv, 11, 61, 75, 155, 161, 166. *See also* Learning communities
Community colleges, xv, 36, 127, 133, 135, 139, 177
Competencies, xiv, 99, 173. *See also* Capacities
Competitive advantage, 30, 141
Complexity, 10, 14, 52, 57, 71, 79, 81, 83, 88, 91, 96, 109, 131, 133, 137, 155, 175, 188
Computer response problem, 2–4, 20–21. *See also* Real problems
Confidentiality, 12, 71, 91, 94, 102, 118
Conflict resolution, 14, 94, 116, 183
Contexts; subcontexts, xiii, xv, xvi, 20, 33, 35–39, 46, 47, 50, 51, 54, 56–59, 62, 64, 71, 72, 75, 77, 78, 83, 85, 103, 104, 105, 126, 151–156, 166. *See also* Biases, context-fed
Corporate universities, xv, 30, 36, 63, 138
Corporations using action learning, 29
Corrigible handicaps, 43
County and municipal, 36. *See also* Government; Henrico County
Creativity, 30, 37, 46, 63, 64, 72, 80
Critical incidents, 51, 52, 96. *See also* Story examples

Critical reflection, 188. *See* Reflection
Cross-cultural awareness, xxi, 146–148, 191
Cross-functional teams, 31, 64, 85, 145, 166, 176
Cross-hierarchical teams, 4, 176
Cultural transformation, 28, 61, 63, 68, 155, 173
Cultures, xv, 13, 21, 22, 23, 31, 38, 47, 50, 54, 56, 61, 62, 64, 71, 72, 73, 77, 78, 85, 103, 106, 107, 108, 109, 126, 133, 146, 147, 159, 163. *See also* Organizational culture
  engineering culture, 61
  executive culture, 61
  monochronic culture, 146
  multicultural, 13, 176
  operator culture, 61
  polychronic culture, 146
Curriculum dominance, 28, 38, 39, 41, 42, 47, 48, 49, 50, 60, 126, 128, 173

Daloz, L. A. P., 153
Debriefing. *See* Action learning debriefing
Dell, 139
Democratic values; democratization, vii, viii, xii, 22, 42, 114, 136, 153. *See also* Action learning descriptive terms
Department of Defense, Senior Service Colleges, 143
Deurinck, G., viii
Dialogue, 9, 10, 11, 22, 23, 53, 79, 92, 96, 124, 143, 188

air time, 79
self-dialogue, 11, 95
Dilworth, R. L., vii, viii, ix, x, xxi, 2–5, 12, 15, 16, 58, 60, 62, 63, 64, 67, 87, 90, 95, 96, 107, 110, 115, 116, 117, 135, 142, 150, 159, 187
Discipline-based assumptions and biases, 45. *See also* Assumptions; Biases
Discipline-based education, 45, 47
Disciplines, 10, 45
  organized bodies of knowledge, 34, 45
Dissonance, 155
Diversity by design, xvi, 13, 22. *See also* Perspectives; Set composition
Domains (environments) for action learning, 35, 36, 39, 45–50, 75, 126–151. *See also* Application domains
Driving forces, xvi, 37, 127, 128, 129, 133, 135, 136, 138, 140–150
Drucker, P., 75

EBO model, 188. *See also* Action learning project models
e-business, xv. *See also* New economy business
e-learning, xv, 38, 46, 49, 51
Empowerment. *See* Power
Engagement, 64, 73, 89, 90, 162, 164, 167. *See also* Participation
Espoused theory vs. theory in use, 72, 129

Index

Ethical behavior; ethical fluency, xii, 33, 71, 111, 166. *See also* Integrity
Expectations, 91, 93, 94, 103, 110, 113, 118, 124, 170, 171
Experimental test, ix, 6, 53, 190
Experts; expertise; expert solutions, xiv, 2, 3, 4, 25, 45, 60, 76, 105, 114, 148, 167, 172, 173, 175
 discipline-based, 45–60
 value of nonexpert thinking, 4, 92

Fabrications of reality, 10
Facilitation, 15, 24, 69, 130, 189
 by invitation or prearrangement only, 25, 183, 189
 self-facilitation, 24, 183
Facilitator, viii, 13, 14, 42, 64, 65, 66, 69, 109, 132, 137, 141, 163, 170. *See also* Learning coach; Mentors; Set advisor
Faculty, adjunct, 133, 134
Failed applications, 16, 57, 58
Familiar problems, settings, and colleagues, 18–20, 71, 188
Federal, 36, 110, 127. *See also* Government
Federal Deposit Insurance Corporation (FDIC), 29, 69
 FDIC Accelerated Decision Making, 69
Federal Executive Institute (FEI), 143
Feedback. *See* System, feedback
Fiorina, C., 106

Firefighters, 20
Flexibility, 27, 61, 145, 166
Florida Atlantic University, Educational Leadership Program, 129
Florida Power and Light, 4, 20. *See also* Power generation problem
Follow-on sets. *See* Implementation linkages
Force field analysis, 127, 136. *See also* Lewin
Fortune, 106
Four squares, 188. *See also* Action learning four squares model
Frames of reference, 174–185
Freedom, xiii, 15, 27, 72, 96, 103, 131, 154, 162, 170, 183
Fresh questions, 6, 12, 16, 31, 32, 40, 59, 68, 76, 114, 161, 167
Future Search Conference, 88

GEC (UK), 85
General Electric (GE), 28, 31, 58, 59, 61, 62, 63, 64, 66–71, 73, 74, 76, 85, 88, 105, 112, 120, 136, 137, 173, 181
 Change Acceleration Program (CAP), 68, 69, 70, 137, 138, 139, 148, 181
 work-out, 28, 58, 61, 63, 64, 66, 67, 68, 88, 120, 148, 181
Gilley, J. and Maycunich, A., 28
Global aspects, 56, 137, 138, 140, 146, 153, 173, 191.

See also Action Learning and Mutual Collaboration Congress; Action learning distribution
Goal determination. *See* Agenda setting
Goldberg, M., 11, 12
Government, 31, 36, 48, 50, 142. *See also* Application domains
  county and municipal, 145, 146
  federal, 142, 143, 144
  state, 144, 145
Gresham's Law, 47
Groove software, 141
Group dynamics, 7, 24, 79, 83, 84, 87, 92, 96, 98, 113, 116, 140, 159, 182
Group (set) norming, 23, 93, 98, 113, 115, 116, 137
Group resume, 93
Guessable gap, 161. *See also* Uncertainty

Habits of
  learning, xv
  mind and thought, 34, 39, 44, 45, 53, 55, 60
  science, 6
  systems thinking, 6. *See also* System
Haigler, K., 135, 136
Hall, C. S. and Lindzey, G., 7
Handy, C., 154
Hawkins, H., 155
Henrico County, 145
Heterarchy. *See* Power
Hewlett-Packard, 106
Hierarchy. *See* Power

Higher education, 36, 60, 62, 115, 128, 129, 132
High-performing workplace. *See* Performance
Hofstede, G., 147
Hofstede's collectivism vs. individualism, 147
"Honest man." *See* Integrity
Honey-Mumford Learning Styles Questionnaire (LSQ), 22, 86, 87
Hospital Intercommunication Study (HIC), 9, 19, 20. *See also* Real problems
HR systems and capability, 28, 99, 145, 150, 151, 181
Human resource development (HRD), xv, 25, 28, 35, 36, 49, 51, 128, 132, 133, 135, 136, 139, 140, 141, 144, 145, 149, 150, 163, 170, 173, 174, 181
  HRD practitioners, 36, 150. *See also* System changers
Hybrid fourth model, 83. *See also* Action learning project models
Hybrid set, 95, 96, 180, 188. *See also* Set composition

IBM, 106
Idolization of perceived past experience, 43, 44, 46
Implementation, 14, 41, 68, 69, 75, 76, 82, 83, 110, 114, 119, 122, 123, 124, 129, 164, 178, 180, 181
Implementation linkages, 14, 76, 83, 120, 122
  follow-on sets, 120–124
Implementation phase (in action

learning cycle), 75, 77, 112, 120, 121, 122
Impulsion to instant activity, 43, 44, 46, 47
Independence, 15. See also Freedom
Individual learning, 69, 126
personal growth and change. See Personal growth
professional and career development, xiii, 90
Influence of group size, 8, 9, 187
Information, 2, 90, 108, 155, 178
Inglis, S., 42
Initial problem statement, 82, 104, 109, 190. See also Problem statement
Initiation phase (in action learning cycle), 74, 77, 78, 103, 104
Inquiry processes, xii, 6, 7, 34, 39, 44, 54, 71, 90, 158, 163, 169, 190
Insights, 1, 11, 32, 37, 39, 47, 51, 53, 54, 63, 64, 92, 95, 119, 134, 152, 156, 157, 164, 169, 187, 190
economic, 165, 166
Instrumental learning, 40, 49, 189
Integrity, 6. See also Ethical behavior
honest communication, 93–94, 156, 185
"honest man," viii, 55
integrity of personal effort, ix
integrity of science, 6
integrity of *Titanic*, 8
Intensity, 5, 30, 67, 88, 120, 131, 158, 159, 161, 188

Interdependence, 55
International organizations and development, 36, 105, 146, 151. See also World
Interpersonal understanding, 141, 165, 190
Intervention by facilitator (learning coach), 14, 15, 17, 25, 97, 157, 189
ITAP International, 96, 187
Iterative nature of action learning, xvi

Janoff, S., 88
Joint project model, 188. See also Action learning project models
Journaling, 168–169. See also Reflective essays; Self-knowledge
Just-in-time learning, xii, 40

Keller, C., 63
Kennedy, W. B., 160
Kerr, J., 63
Kerr, S., 63, 64
Knapp, A., 26
Knowledge creation, 46. See also Learning yields; Yields
Knowles, M., 26–28
Kodak, 30
Kuhn, T. S., 33

Lanahan, E. D. and Maldonado, L., 69
Last chance parolees, 24, 25
Leader control of learning, xii, 38, 46, 47, 48, 49, 50, 132, 169
Leaderless sets; learner control of learning, xi, 23, 41, 132,

156, 184. *See also* Set composition
Leadership and executive development, xiii, 29, 59, 63, 67, 68, 69, 70, 73, 74, 85, 131, 139, 143
Leadership in International Management (LIM), 16, 70
Learner involvement, 184. *See also* Engagement
Learner maturity, 24, 177, 185
Learner readiness, 26, 27
Learning, 1, 11, 47, 53, 60, 70, 71, 96, 123, 125, 150, 151, 156, 160, 162, 167, 171, 173, 175, 187, 190
  consequences, viii, 6
  continuous; lifelong, xi, 31, 126, 133, 134, 149, 167, 173, 185
  co-terminus with life, xi, 26
  cultures, 174
  deep; internalized, xii, 51, 52, 81, 92, 161
  experiential, xv, 54
  formal, xi, 28, 60, 126, 128, 129, 133, 136, 139, 143, 144, 146, 147, 174, 189
  gaps, 121, 123
  goals, 16. *See also* Agenda setting
  holistic, 13
  informal, xi
  motivation, xii, 27, 37, 59, 68, 133
  as priority over task focus, 12, 15, 131, 138
  at rate of change, xv, 17, 18, 19, 51
  about self, viii, 6, 52, 157, 165. *See also* Self-knowledge
  strategies, xiii, 27, 28, 31, 86
  technology-based learning. *See* Learning on the fly
  transformational. *See* Transformative learning
  about value systems. *See* Beliefs; Value systems
Learning coach, 11, 14, 15, 17, 21, 24, 25, 42, 86, 97, 98, 102, 103, 104, 108, 111, 112, 116, 117, 120, 137, 141, 144, 157, 179, 180, 182, 188–189. *See also* Facilitator; Set advisor
Learning communities, xii, 51, 85, 176
Learning curve, 18, 19
Learning equation. *See* Action learning equation
Learning experience; learning event, 15, 27, 81, 90, 93, 142, 170
Learning guarantees, 38, 40, 47, 48, 49, 50
Learning how to learn, 11, 29, 52, 131, 149, 159, 160
Learning logs; journals, 21, 53, 95, 168, 169, 180
Learning maps, 22
Learning on the fly, 38, 40, 46, 47, 48, 49, 50. *See* e-learning
Learning organization, 19, 31, 149, 173. *See also* Organizational learning
Learning style differences, 22, 27, 85, 86, 114, 167, 176
Learning support systems, 51
Learning with and from each other, vii, xi, 6, 52
Learning yields, xiii, 19, 85,

132, 184. *See also* Outcomes; Yields
Lewin, K., xii, 7, 123, 127
Lewin's field theory of personality, 7. *See also* Force field analysis
Lindeman, E., xi, 25–28
Livingston, J., 57
Low-hanging fruit, 65
Lucinsky, J., 168

Management Institute of Lund (MIL), 69, 70, 71
concepts of leadership, 70
Management support, 3, 14, 31, 57, 58, 67, 73, 82, 106, 108, 175, 178, 182
Manchester hospital merger, NHS project, 20, 21, 23, 86–88, 114–115, 159
Marquardt, M., xiii, 11, 17, 29, 56, 62, 78
Marsick, V. and Cederholm, L., 69, 70
May, G., 140
Meaning making, 11, 15, 27, 34, 70, 166, 184
Meister, J., 30, 138, 139
Memorandum of understanding, 90, 91, 97–101, 116, 118, 177, 178, 180, 181
Mental models. *See* Mindsets
Mentors; mentorship, viii, 97, 144, 158
Metamorphosis, 160
Metaphor, 87, 155, 160, 163, 167, 168
Mezirow, J., 27, 28, 60, 152, 158, 166
Mezirow's theory of transformative learning, 166. *See also* Mezirow
Millbrook Distribution Services, 140
Mindsets; mental models, xvi, 32, 33, 34, 38, 39, 41, 43, 44, 45, 52, 58, 145, 149. *See also* Assumptions; Biases; Worldviews
Model characteristics, general, 78
Model I (MI), 72
Morgan, G., 33, 38
Motivation. *See* Learning, motivation
Motorola University, 139
Mulgan, G., 33
Multicultural, 146–148, 176. *See also* Cultures
Mumford, A., 10, 13, 16
Municipal. *See* Government
Mutual collaboration, vii, 6, 11, 93, 119, 162

Nadler, L., 28
National Health Service (NHS), 87. *See also* Manchester hospital merger
National Training Center (NTC), 143. *See also* U.S. Army
Nee, E., 106
New economy business; e-business, xv, 36, 127, 140–141. *See also* Virtual organization
Nongovernment organizations (NGOs)—xv, 36, 147, 148. *See also* World
Nonprofit organizations, 31, 36, 141

OPFOR (military opposing forces maneuvers), 143
Optima Award, 145
Organic growth, 172
Organizational acceptance, xiii, xvi, 29, 30, 33, 34, 38, 42, 43, 44, 45, 48, 50, 53, 57, 70, 132, 138, 153
Organizational capacity, 85. *See also* Organizational development; Organizational learning
Organizational culture, 23, 31, 56, 57, 58, 59, 63, 75, 77, 83, 85, 88, 104, 106, 107, 110, 126, 145, 148, 177, 182
Organizational development and change, xiv, xxi, xxii, 10, 34, 36, 62, 63, 68, 71, 73, 74, 107, 148, 149, 157, 185
Organizational impact. *See* Outcomes; Yields
Organizational learning, xiii, 29, 30, 31, 61, 149. *See also* Learning organization
Osborne's laboratories of democracy, 145
Outcomes, 45, 51–53, 73–74, 108, 115, 119, 120–121, 156–158, 161–162, 190
 control of, 41, 42
 interpersonal; group, 35, 52–53, 89, 114, 166
 organizational, 51, 58, 62, 67–68, 70, 73, 124
 personal, 51–52, 89, 166, 171
 unpredictable variety, 1, 33, 39, 89, 132, 161, 166–167, 171, 184

Ownership, xi, 14. *See also* Problem ownership

P (programmed knowledge). *See* Learning equation
paradigms, 15, 44, 60, 108, 123, 140, 173
Participation, 9, 14, 27
 mandatory, 74, 182
 value when client joins set, xvi, 14, 73, 89, 90, 116, 124, 158, 163
 voluntary, 14, 74, 181
Past experience, 10, 27. *See also* Idolization of perceived past experience
Pedagogy, 26, 60, 135
Pedler, M., 11
Perceptions, xi, 10, 27, 51, 52, 97, 107, 109
Performance, 173, 183, 185, 186
Personal growth; maturity, 11, 22, 34, 51, 59, 70, 90, 95, 157. *See also* Individual learning; Story examples
Personnel Journal, 145
Perspectives; perspective change, viii, 12, 22, 35, 46, 51, 52, 68, 89, 98, 114, 152, 160, 163, 165, 166, 168, 176
 total systems perspective, 124
Phases. *See* Action learning cycle and phases; Action learning phase; Implementation phase; Initiation phase
Pilot programs, 58, 73, 129, 133
Pitfalls, xiii, 89, 178
Political sensitivity, 180
Potts, M., 63
Power, 61, 67, 82, 90, 148, 156, 161

Index

base, xiv, 61
distribution, xiv, 47, 58, 61
empowerment, enabling, xiv, 3, 8, 13, 27, 56, 57, 58, 65, 67, 72, 74, 90, 103, 106, 145, 174
heterarchical, xiv, 61
hierarchical, xiv, 31, 56, 58, 61, 85, 136
position power, 149
power of championed decisions, 67, 68
win-lose, 61
Power generation problem, 4, 5
Precautions, 92–93, 101
Presentations to client. *See* Action learning presentations
Private sector. *See* Businesses and related services
Problem and project complexity. *See* Complexity
Problem clarification, 91, 103, 109
Problem ownership, xiii, 76, 83, 84, 122, 163. *See also* Ownership
Problems. *See* Real problems; Unfamiliar problems
Problem solving, xii, 3, 4, 5, 11, 12, 15, 17, 29, 30, 31, 38, 43, 47, 55, 57, 59, 60, 61, 62, 69, 71, 74, 84, 131, 137, 145, 161, 167
Problem statement, 82, 103, 104, 109, 110, 113, 115, 117, 178, 190
Problem unfamiliarity. *See* Unfamiliar problems
Process mapping, 64
Productivity, 2, 8, 108

Professional and career development, xiii, 29, 160
Programmed knowledge, 187. *See also* Action learning equation
Pygmalion effect, 57

Q (questioning insight). *See* Action learning equation
Quality circles, 19
Quest, xi, 8, 40, 157
Questioning insight, 189. *See also* Action learning equation
Questions, 11, 16, 38, 39, 53, 65, 69, 96, 123, 154, 157, 160, 164, 169, 189. *See also* Action learning equation, Q; Fresh questions

Rate of change, xv, 17–19
Rate of learning, 17–19, 149
Rationality of decision making in uncertainty, 72
Real problems, viii, xii, 1, 6, 11, 14, 15, 51, 52, 55, 57, 63, 64, 70, 73, 76, 79, 96, 109, 130, 131, 133, 137, 138, 140, 154, 157, 162, 187, 189
Army truck problem, 5, 20, 21
Belgian project, viii. *See also* Belgian project
computer response problem, 2–4
firefighter problem, 20
Hospital Intercommunication Study, 9, 19, 20
Manchester hospital merger,

20–21, 86, 87. *See also* Manchester hospital merger
power generation problem, 4, 5
Titanic, 7, 8
Reflection; reflective process, xiii, 7, 11, 16, 17, 21, 22, 28, 32, 35, 41, 44, 49, 53, 54, 63, 68, 69, 70, 92, 94, 95, 96, 97, 108, 121, 123, 124, 125, 143, 152, 153, 157, 158, 159, 161, 163, 169, 172, 175, 180, 185, 188
  balance with action, xii. *See also* Action
  critical reflection, xiii, 11, 21, 22, 54, 55, 96, 114, 187, 188, 190
  critical self-reflection, 7, 152, 159
  nonlinearity, 53
Reflective essays, 27, 96, 156, 160, 163, 167. *See also* Story examples; Self-organizing
Relationship-building, 146. *See also* Set cohesion
Responsibilities, 100, 152, 169–170, 190. *See also* Working team agreement
Restraining forces, xvi, 37, 127, 128, 129, 133, 135, 136, 138, 140–150
Results. *See* Outcomes; Yields
Revans, R. W., x, 1, 6–10, 12, 15–19, 24, 34, 43, 44, 45, 46, 47, 54, 55, 63, 64, 65, 68, 70, 71, 76, 79, 82, 85, 102, 109, 118, 122, 123, 131, 143, 152, 153, 156, 157, 158, 160, 161, 165, 172, 173, 183, 185, 187, 188, 189, 190
  corrigible handicaps, 43
  father of action learning, 1
Revans Institute for Action Learning and Research, 29, 130
Rice University, 128
Risk-taking; risk-aversion, 62, 63, 68, 84, 130, 131, 132, 134, 165, 184
Robust applications, 174
Rohlin, T., 70
Romania, 141
Rommel, E., 7

Salem Company, 135
Scenarios, ix, xxii, 143
Schein, E., 61, 62
Schön, D., 13
Schumacher, E. E., 8
Science of uncertainties, 155. *See also* Uncertainty
Scientific discovery; scientific method, ix, 6, 118, 190
Self, viii, 52, 54, 89, 155, 157, 159, 190
Self-directed work teams, 23, 136, 175. *See also* Team building; Teamwork
Self-efficacy; self-confidence, xi, 29, 30, 52, 73, 85, 103, 131, 134, 162, 163, 165, 170
Self-image, 186
Self-knowledge; self-discovery, 54, 55, 156, 157, 161, 165, 190
Self-ordering; self-organizing,

Index

169, 185. *See also* Leaderless sets
Senge, P., 173
Senior Executive Service of FEI, 143
Senior Service Colleges, DOD, 143
Service learning, 128
Set advisor, viii, 14, 24. *See also* Learning coach
Set cohesion and continuity, 14, 23, 79, 83, 84, 89, 167
Set composition; set diversity, 13, 22, 84–87, 91, 95–98, 112, 113, 114, 133, 159, 167, 176, 180, 187, 188, 189
Sets. *See* Action learning sets
Shared vision, 22
Silence for reflection, 95
Simulations, 10, 30, 137, 154, 189
Six Sigma, 181
Skill accrual, 40
Slater, R., 64
Small businesses, 36, 105, 141, 142, 146
Social work, xv, 129
Speed. *See* Velocity
Spontaneity, xi, 45, 95
Sprint University, 139
State. *See* Government
Stewart, T. A., 61
Stogdill, R. M., 78
Story examples, 2–5, 7–9, 24, 25, 81–82, 159–165
Strategic goals, priorities, 174
Stress and its control, 179
Synergy, xix, 11, 21, 79, 142, 146
System. *See also* System Alpha; System Beta; System Gamma
chaos theory, 155
cybernetics, ix, 10
dynamics, 7
evolutionary HRD, xxii
feedback, viii, 35, 79
general system theory and theorists, 10
system complexity. *See* Complexity
systemic problems, 58
systemic shortfall, 2
system of values, viii. *See also* Value systems
system variety. *See* Variety
thinking, xviii, xxii, 6, 166. *See also* Perspectives
turnaround, 4
System Alpha, 6, 7, 16, 55, 110, 118, 157, 165, 185, 189–190
System Beta, 6, 7, 36, 37, 48, 50, 55, 118, 157, 165, 185, 190
System changers, 148. *See also* Application domains
System Gamma, 6, 7, 34, 45, 55, 156, 157, 165, 185, 190

Tacit knowledge, 17, 53, 154, 167
Task focus, 184
Task force, 4, 16, 125, 138, 174, 175
Team building, 29, 141. *See also* Cross-functional teams; Cross-hierarchical teams
Teamwork; team learning, 59, 83, 84, 96, 100, 103

Techniques, ix, 10, 21, 93, 102, 173
Technology (computer-based), xii, 2–4
  information, 2
  solo-operated, xii
  technology-mediated content, 51. *See also* Learning on the fly
  veil of, 52
Thomason, J. J., 8
Tichy, N. M. and Sherman, S., 63, 68
Timeliness, xii, xiv
Timid applications, 174
Titanic, 7, 8
Transfer of learning, 183
Transformative learning; transformation, 13, 27, 152, 153, 155, 156, 157, 158, 159, 163, 165, 166, 170, 171, 185, 190
  Mezirow's theory, 166
Truck problem, 5, 20, 21
True start point, 108
Trust, 6, 12, 15, 30, 34, 57, 70, 71, 84, 95, 96, 97, 107, 156, 170
Trust the process, 132, 133
Tuckman, B. W. and Jensen, M. A. C., 93, 117

Uncertainty; unpredictability, 1, 5, 6, 15, 18, 30, 34, 43, 52, 53, 59, 70, 91, 132, 154, 184
  uncertainty logic, 1
  uncertainty science, 155
Undiscussability in climate of fear, 72
Unfamiliar problems, settings, and colleagues, 6, 9, 12, 15, 18, 19, 27, 31, 59, 64, 71, 76, 80, 81, 86, 112, 122, 131, 154, 160, 175, 185
Unfreezing, 32, 123. *See also* Lewin
Universities using action learning, 29
Unlearning, 44
U.S. Army, xxi, 5, 7, 143

Value matrix (GE), 65, 66
Value systems, viii, 10, 190. *See also* Beliefs
Variety, 33, 98, 154, 170. *See also* Set composition
Velocity, 18, 19, 41, 189. *See also* Learning, at rate of change
Virginia Department of Transportation, 144
Virtual business, 140
Virtual corporate universities, 139
Virtual organization; virtuality, 139, 191
Virtual teams, 140, 141
Virtual workplace, 183
Von Glinow, M. A., 63

Washington Post, 62, 63
Watson, T., 106
Weinstein, K., 39
Weisbord, M., xii, 9, 25, 88, 127
Welch, J., 59, 61, 63, 64
Willis, V. J., vii, viii, ix, x, xxii, 11, 12, 15, 60, 73, 76, 83, 89, 90, 95, 112, 116, 117, 118, 119, 122,

149, 150, 158, 159, 162, 163, 164, 167
Wisdom, viii, xiii, 7, 73, 154, 159, 172
Working team agreement, 23, 93, 94, 97, 98, 106, 115
Work-out. *See* General Electric
World, 36, 48, 50, 146, 155. *See also* Application domains

World Trade Center, 153, 154
Worldviews, 45, 160. *See also* Mindsets
Wyatt, F., 168

Yields, 186. *See also* Learning yields; Outcomes
Yorks, L., O'Neill, J., and Marsick, V., 11